NEW RUSSIAN PLAYS

NEW RUSSIAN PLAYS

Translated and edited by

NOAH BIRKSTED-BREEN

YURI KLAVDIEV

NATALIA KOLIADA

MAKSIM KUROCHKIN

NATALIA MOSHINA

VLADIMIR ZUEV

SPUTNIK

CONTENTS

SLOW SWORD   1
Yuri Klavdiev

DREAMS   69
Natalia Koliada

TITYUS THE IRREPROACHABLE   105
Maksim Kurochkin

TECHNIQUES OF BREATHING IN AN   165
    AIRLOCKED SPACE
Natalia Moshina

MUMS   197
Vladimir Zuev

PERFORMANCE NOTES   230

ABOUT THE AUTHORS *&* TRANSLATOR   231

THE SLOW SWORD

by

Yuri Klavdiev

I. THE NEWS OF THE DAY

An office. The colour scheme is blue and white. The clerk Alexei keeps walking around the office and back to his desk, like everyone else.

Enters.

Vlad Hi. Hi . . . Hi.

– (*Female voice*) Hi. Alexei! Hi. Listen, did I do this one yesterday? I can't remember . . .

(People are walking all over the place, shifting paper, talking on the phone. The surveillance cameras are switched on. The clerk Alexei moves his lips.)

Vlad I've already seen him. He looks odd. I saw him on the bus because we take the same route in. Oh, hi! How's things?

– Cool.

Vlad You've got a great tan! Where'd you go?

– Thanks for the compliment but . . . from a solarium . . .

Vlad Yeah? Absolutely couldn't tell . . . no really, I mean, damn . . . No really it's cool . . . Totally convincing. How's things?

– (*Male voice: practically only moving his lips*) Amazing . . . (*Half-whispering*) I'm out of here in a month. I haven't told anyone. Don't tell anyone yet, okay? I want to see the whole place fall apart. But it's true, though, no? Imagine it, I leave and in, like, two weeks everything will fall to bits. Just like that, really, the company, it's like, anything can happen. You . . . well I can't *not* leave, well you see what I'm saying, I just can't stay, and I'm not the only one, either . . .

Vlad Yeah? Shit, it's good you warned me. Shit, thanks . . . yeah, better look at other stuff just to be safe. Mm-hm.

(Their desks.)

(The clerk Alexei is by the threshold of his desk.)

Vlad Yes, wicked. *I will definitely leave, I've been looking for something else my whole life. Talk to me.* Hello. Hi, yes . . . hi. Oh, hi. Thank you. *There are so many of us. Everyone has four fucking mobiles, full of such utter shit that it's fucking hard to believe. We use something like thirty numbers in all but we add more and more to the phone's memory every month.*

We take down information from notices

We send things to each other

Whatever doesn't fit in the phone, we carry around with us on bits of paper in our wallets. There are so many of us, we can't keep everyone in mind.

(He sits down at the table.)

Vlad So . . . what have we got? To whom do we need to be grateful? *(He takes a sticker off his computer)* Right . . .

(He lifts his hand and touches his forehead with the crumpled paper. He puts the paper into the pot of fragrance.)

Vlad The management, the management, the management.

(Three bits of paper. He cuts them with a knife and puts them in the same pot.)

Vlad And the boss again.

(Into the same pot.)

Vlad *(aloud, loudly)* Yulia! Can I talk to you for a second?

– coming! Give me two seconds!

(He puts the knife back, hiding it somewhere under the table.)

Vlad No, it's nothing too serious, there was a note for you here that's all. Listen it seems that your subscription to *Hustler* was cancelled for lack of funds on the account. The fact that you're a long-time subscriber is no longer a valid justification . . . because you haven't paid for the last three years. But, as soon as you pay what you owe, they'll happily start delivering again, including the issues which you've been missing!

(They run off, laughing. He comes back. He sits at his desk again.)

〜

Vlad (*working on his computer*) Right . . . right . . . fuck this . . . and this . . . come here . . . right . . . fuck this . . . where's that? Right . . . what the fuck is this . . .? Where did you come from? Come on, you bitch, come on. Beat them up, cat, beat them up! . . . come on, damn it . . . oh, wicked! . . . fantastic! . . . yeah . . . fuck off . . . fuck you . . . Whoa! . . . whoa, whoa, hey, have you crashed, or something? Well, you sodding . . . Well, fuck you . . . right . . . right . . . What's this? Download, bitch! . . . motherfucker . . . Right . . . yeah, yeah, yy-ee-aah . . . come on . . . come on . . . good boy . . . excellent . . . now let me onto the Internet . . . right . . . excellent . . . come on . . . wicked . . . 115 KB . . . damn . . . whatever . . . come on . . . right . . . keep looking, pal . . . right . . . what's that? What is that? So, give me *that* one then. And that one, and that one . . .

(He waits for the sites to download. He digs around in the papers on his desk, reaches for a toothpick.)

Vlad Cool . . . that's a lot of data. Shit . . . a whole fucking lot of data . . . leave me here, commander, I'll shoot myself, I promise . . . please. Bastard, I can't kill you, I've only got one bullet. And you won't give it to me, you whore. You bitch, you're not giving it to me, whore . . .

(He hits his computer, hysterically.)

Vlad (*looks up from the screen*) Hi. Wow . . . You look great! Amazing . . . is it new? Listen . . . do you want a coffee? Yeah, I think we can. We've already done an hour and I've already done the most important things . . . just let me save it all, ok?

– Yeah, okay. I'll wait for you there . . .

(They drink tea together, standing besides the water cooler.)

Vlad Someone's phone was on the blink. Can you tell Marina, yeah? How's things this week?

– Well, it's only just started. Hey, is it true that Roma's quitting?

Vlad Seems like he wants to go in two weeks. Will you tell Marina?

– About Roma? She already knows.

Vlad No. About the water. It's running out. Today the tea's alright, thank God . . . but I remember a few days ago it like hardly had any taste . . . And there was this white scum in the cup . . .

– I'll tell Marina.

Vlad *Then I started thinking that we're getting old but we don't notice it. It's just at certain moments when time suddenly shoots forward. And suddenly we see we're older.*

– So he told you himself, he's definitely leaving, yeah?

Vlad *Some people are even dying. They just sit under the light of the moon, by the river, and then one dies but the other only notices that in the morning.* Alyona, what do you think – will he betray us big time at the meeting? But I'm serious though – I just found out today. From him.

– Let them sort it out themselves.

Vlad See you later, I need to go to the um . . . well, the loo, basically. . .

(He shuts the loo door. He leaves and sits at his computer. A girl comes over to him.)

– We've got a birthday coming up. Are you joining us? It's tomorrow evening. At five.

Vlad Are we going to club together – how much?

– Hundred and fifty. If you've got more, give more.

Vlad Whose is it?

– It's a secret. Are you coming?

Vlad Definitely. *(He gets his wallet)* Here's two hundred for the secret.

– Cool. See you, tomorrow, then. Dress code: free-style.

*. . . Taking place at the same time, in another place, for example
– the communal ground floor to any block of flats. The walls
are battered, they haven't been painted for a long time. Written
on the wall: ACCEPT, MOTORHEAD, AAAAA – GO AND
FUCK YOURSELVES!!!! VICA THE WHORE SUCKED OFF AN
ARMENIAN. There are two people, a bloke and a girl. The bloke sits
on the stairs, the girl is on the floor. She's got her back to the window.
Her trouser leg is torn up, her legs are covered with jab-marks, her
lips are trembling, there's a syringe in her hands, a stream of blood
flows down her leg, and another stream flows into the first . . . and
it's like when autumn leaves fall and are forgotten because nobody
needs them, though they are as beautiful as the stars. . .*

Bloke The main thing is – not to hurry. Don't hurry. You've *got*
veins. You can't *not* have them.

Girl Shit . . . (*She rubs her leg forcefully, winces from the pain
because she touches the sore spots.*) Shit. . .

Bloke Don't hurry. The main thing's – not to hurry. The ancient
Hindus also lived till thirty – but no more, and that's because
they were injecting themselves. Yoga's a pile of rubbish. They just
started mucking around at some point. Because their coffee wasn't
having any effect any more. . .

Girl (*rubbing her leg*) Shit. . .

Bloke And then the Chinese came, gave them opium, and
captured them all . . .

Girl (*rubbing her leg*) Ow. . .

Bloke The Hindus – shit, man . . . we had one Uzbek working with
us. He took a box and starts fucking about, throwing it around
the warehouse like a stupid fucker. "Vere vill I put eet?" "Hey, vere
will I put eet?!" Fucking tosser. Imagine that, everything's ordered
specially by the labels, it's not fucking possible *not* to know where
things go. He spent half a year learning what goes where. Thick as
a cunt . . . (*he sighs*) . . . just like the Hindus. . .

Girl (*rubbing her leg, jabbing her leg with the syringe; for some
time she digs around in her leg*) Fuck. . .

The bloke lies on the floor. He puts some sun glasses in front of his face and looks at them as if into a mirror. He squeezes the vein on his neck.

Bloke That's the philosophy they have. Sit there and keep sitting. Everyone will come to you and explain what's what. You don't need to do anything. That's the main difference with our country and with our philosophy. (*Without taking his hands from his vein, he takes the top off the syringe with his teeth and inserts the syringe in his vein.*)

Girl (*rubbing her leg, hits it with her hand, stamps her leg, hides the syringe in her pocket and bangs on the wall*) Shit! Shit! Shit!

The bloke, having injected himself, stretches out blissfully.

Girl Hey, you're feeling really good, there, yeah? Yuri, come on, help me, what are you doing, I've got problems here, shit. . .

Bloke Quit whining. Girl, stop! Sit quietly, everything's cool, come on then. . .

He goes over to the girl, lowers her trouser leg, kissing every sore.

Girl Okay, er, what are you . . .

Bloke Ssh. Ssh. Ssh. Enough. The main thing is to calm down. Everything's okay. "Nothing is impossible" – have you seen that advert?

He rolls up her sleeve.

Girl Man, I haven't got any veins in my arm anymore! Where are you going?

Bloke . . . sssssssh . . . You have to treat your organism in the right way . . . what lovely autumn leaves. They're lovely because nobody needs them. They just fall. And sometimes people fall into *them* and that's nice for everyone because there are whole piles of them, and they just *are*, just like stars. . .

He kisses the girl.

Girl Is this a type of spell, yeah?

Bloke No. It's so you relax. And so people understand that they just *are*. Even the leaves are more important because they're beautiful.

The bloke kisses her hand and sits opposite her, closing his eyes. He runs the tips of his fingers over the surface of her hand. He suddenly grabs her wrist and squeezes it tightly. Opening his eyes wide, he inserts the syringe. He injects her.

Girl Ah...

Bloke Sssssh...

For some time, both sit still, opposite each other. Then they lean in towards each other. Then they kiss. The bloke feels the girl all over, as if in a dream, and she does the same with him. Tenderly kissing the nape of the neck, running tongues across skin, feeling each other's every finger, – they make these same movements over and over, constantly starting from the beginning because the beginning does not exist for them. They slowly crawl under each other's jeans, leaning their heads onto each other's shoulders. They fall asleep.

Girl (*lifting her head*) How did that happen?!

Bloke You need to know the places...

Girl Why can't *I* find them?

Bloke Because you don't know what you need. The human organism is not an idiot. It doesn't just open up like that, open sesame. We're thinking beings, Yulia. We have to move forward.

Girl And you, like, are moving forward?

Bloke I'm, like, moving forward... I'm not a Hindu, a white man won't bring me anything on a saucer. I haven't shat on my own culture. I wasn't like those yogis, sticking my leg up my own nose while the radio and the steamboat and the television were being invented for me...

Girl And what do you practice?

Bloke I study the world.

Girl What for?

Bloke If you know how things work, you can hit your vein with your eyes closed.

Girl Only for that?

Bloke It's a start. It's already something. If I were you, I'd just listen very carefully to what I'm saying.

Girl Do you . . . despise me or something?

Bloke Nah. I feel sorry for you. For practically everyone.

Girl Why?

Bloke Because heroine wasn't invented for people like you. It was thought up for supermen. To help them reach the stars.

Girl You're a superman, I suppose?

Bloke Not yet.

Girl But why is it not allowed then?

Bloke It is. It's allowed. Do you remember Kolya?

Girl The one who deals grass.

Bloke He used to deal. He's in prison now.

Girl I didn't know. . .

Bloke You're always hanging round your house, that's why. You never go outside. But a person has to move around, that's what I'm saying.

Girl So what's with Kolya? So, he's in prison, *and*?

Bloke And do you remember Vitaly? Who's actually Vasya?

Girl Who also deals grass?

Bloke Used to deal. He's also in prison.

Girl What about it?

Bloke Can you see the system? Everyone who deals in grass is put in jail. But I've got a mate who deals heroin, they just let them out of jail. The cops seriously let them out. Is that normal?

Girl Is someone in the government on our side? Someone's a drug-addict?

Bloke That's a wicked idea . . . maybe. I don't think so, though. Or they would have made absolutely everything legal a long time ago. Just heroine's a good way of separating people who want to reach the stars and people who just want to get fucked.

Girl How do you separate them?

Bloke The ones who want to reach the stars – they don't get involved in shit.

Girl You're talking rubbish . . . they steal, they're rats . . .

Bloke Not all of them are rats. There are rats everywhere. Well, they steal. Have they stolen from you, or something? They steal from whoever has something worth fucking off with.

Girl Fuck yeah, the path to the stars . . .

Bloke It's all true – us lot, we've got no fucking need for possessions. And it's still better than being a moron from MTV. Shit, when I see Kelly Osbourne . . . it's the worst fucking thing . . .

Girl Who needs them? The stars?

Bloke The people on the other side. Old people. They think about us . . . sometimes we make them sad.

Girl Why does it make them sad?

Bloke We don't see what they see. We're just running, running . . . doing stuff.

Girl And you – you're not doing stuff.

Bloke Nah. Why?

Girl Well . . . so what do you want to do?

Bloke Anything I feel like. For now finding my vein. And then I'll go to a film. And then I'll read a book. And then I'll go to Siberia. Forever.

Girl Why?

Bloke It's nearer to the stars.

Girl Why's that then?

Bloke No politicians there. People don't even have electricity. That's why they don't watch television. And so they don't get tricked.

Girl Why are you still here then?

Bloke I'm looking for someone to go with. I'll get bored by myself.

Girl Wicked . . . how about me?

Bloke Not yet.

Girl Why?

Bloke You're not ready yet. When you reach the stars, they'll ask you – "Why are you here?"

Girl Who'll ask?

Bloke Old people. They live up there, in the stars.

Girl Who?

Bloke Old people. Who gave their lives to becoming the cosmos. Morrison, Picasso, Copernicus, Vivaldi . . .

Girl So wait, did they all shoot up?

Bloke Some only smoked . . . doesn't matter. You don't have to be a druggie to reach the stars. What matters is that you answer when they ask you.

Girl And how will you answer?

Bloke I'll say that . . . I'll say . . . Yulia?

Girl What?

Bloke Would you suck my dick?

Girl Why?

Bloke Well, do you remember we were mucking around at Alyonka's? When your bloke went away? And we shut ourselves in the room and . . . and your bloke called and someone told him you'd already gone out. And then your friend also called and told him you were already sleeping . . . and we were doing somersaults . . . Damn, it was so cool. . .

Girl You liked it?

Bloke Yeeeah . . . let's do the same now?

Girl But what if someone passes by?

Bloke They don't give a fuck . . . well, they pass by, what are they going to do anyway? Call the police? Do they really give that much of a fuck? We can always get dressed and go. And they'll be left, like a fucker. . .

Girl Why like a fucker?

Bloke Because they dreamed their whole life of someone doing that to them. They all watch porn at night and imagine the same thing happening . . . but us – we're different. You and me – we're free . . . we can go to the stars – easily.

Girl Freedom – is sucking someone off on the stairs, yeah? So you can only get to the stars via a cock, or are there any other ways?

Bloke Well, if you don't want to, you don't have to . . . forget it, I'm off. (*He gets up.*)

Girl Hey, where are you going?

Bloke I'm going to read a book. Until it kicks in . . . Yulia?

Girl What?

Bloke Freedom is you. You and nobody else. When you're like that, come and get me, we'll go to Siberia! (*He leaves.*)

The girl huddles over to the warm radiator and falls asleep.

II. VLAD

Vlad's in a room. Next to him is Alla.

Alla Hi!

Vlad Hi.

Alla How's things over here?

Vlad Fine.

Alla Hey what's wrong? Why are you unhappy? Oh dear, oh dear, who's upset my little one? . . . (*She embraces Vlad. He smiles, unhappily.*) Well, that's enough, sweetheart, come on now . . . Let's be positive, make an effort! . . .

Vlad No, really, everything's fine. . .

Alla Hm. That sour face can only mean one thing. In our day and age – that a person's been fired from his job. Is that it?

Vlad No, no . . . definitely not . . .

Alla Stress, then? Draw your boss, chew it up and spit it out . . .

Vlad What?

Alla The Japanese thought that one up. It helps me.

Vlad And if life has fucked you up?

Alla What?

Vlad If life has fucked you up? What do you chew then?

Alla Then chew a newspaper. Just don't get poisoned by the lead. The ink is harmful.

Vlad Is there any adequate prescription?

Alla Let's eat and go somewhere. I've got a couple of hours till yoga, we could go and drink bio-yoghurt.

Vlad Bio-yoghurt won't help. Alla, I've got a question for you . . .

Alla Okay. Only then we go for bio-yoghurt. Deal?

Vlad Fine.

Alla Where shall we go? We can go to *Vogue*™ but you go up the fucking wall waiting for a table. Everyone does yoga today, so everyone goes there first. Or *NeoLife*™ . . . but it's better to go somewhere with a white room – it's healthier for something, white's the colour of the womb in the baby's imagination, they associate it with the mother . . . there was something about a whale, too, something like whales only see everything in white. So . . .

Vlad Wait. My question.

Alla Oh, okay.

Vlad Today I was observing myself all day. I can tell you everything about my day. . .

Alla No need for that. I'm not ready for that level of detail. Especially because. . .

Vlad Well? What?

Alla . . . Especially because it was the same for me. We do exactly the same job – are you forgetting that? Just in different places. We're workers of competing agencies.

Vlad Right, let's start there. If your company drives mine out – what happens?

Alla We'll be in the market instead of you.

Vlad And if mine does that?

Alla Then *we* won't be in the market.

Vlad And if someone else's does it?

Alla Then neither of us stays. Vlad, I'm starting to wonder, did you buy your diploma on the metro?

Vlad No. But, actually, what if I had?

Alla Had what?

Vlad Well, what if I'd bought my diploma on the metro? Then what?

Alla Nothing. But you didn't buy it, did you? Vlad, what are you driving at?

Vlad What are we here for? The market – what's it for? We both go to work every God-given day, Alla . . . God created the world the whole world. The universe. Light. Darkness. The whole fucking thing. Evil. Good. Every type of filth – and now he spends his life smoking. It's totally fine. I'm not complaining. He's cool. He deserved it.

Alla Have you been hanging out with the Jehovah's Witnesses or something? Vlad. You gotta be careful. Zhanka told me they take people's flats away from them...

Vlad I'm not talking about that. I'm talking about us. I started working in my first year at university. Now I'm twenty-five. And now what?

Alla Well, what?

Vlad Nothing, that's the point! What have I done? What have I got? You can love God, or not love God, you can burn churches and spit in the Bible but he created the world. He CREATED THE WORLD!!! And me?

Alla (*as if a metro announcement*) Attention please! Middle-age crises are beginning this season earlier than usual! Attention! You are requested to take away from your boyfriends: all alcohol, dangerous razors, sleeping pills, to seal up your ovens, window frames, and throw out the laces from all boots! We request those of adventurous spirit to go out into nature and fuck as necessary!

Vlad Alla, do you understand what I'm saying?

Alla Of course. You're not happy with yourself. It happens. It's fine. The most important thing in your life you've already achieved– you're independent, you earn more than five thousand dollars a month...

Vlad Is that enough?

Alla Of course.

Vlad It's enough for the bio-yoghurt, I suppose? Everything's for that?

Alla What do you mean *everything*?

Vlad Copernicus, dammit! Bloody Michelangelo! Fucking Fassbinder! Everything!

Alla What about Copernicus? They've done everything already. They would have envied us. In the Middle Ages, they'd have quartered people for a microwave. The Inquisition...

Vlad Alla, have you any idea what you're saying?

Alla Vlad, I think it's better if I go, okay? You're depressed and I'm not really up for all of this. It kills me. I'm not going out with you for *this*. I want a normal relationship, without all this bollocks, without anything.

Vlad I. Want. To. Understand. Why. We. Live.

Alla We live a normal life, we've got money and a roof over our heads. What else do we need? We don't need anything else.

Vlad Are you sure?

Alla One hundred percent. I grew up just me and mum. I know for sure that all this bollocks about meaning and purpose are just . . . bollocks. Nobody needs anything. Well, that's not right. You need to fuck and talk. That's what everyone needs. My mum was just the same. She always had people over at night. I was little, they made me go to bed and were talking in the kitchen until three in the morning. And then I woke up in the night for a drink of water, I went to the kitchen and they're all just fucking there. Just like that. Your whole intellectual capability is there to pick up girls. That's all.

Vlad That's not true. I mean, obviously, it is as well, but . . . it's not true. There's the cosmos. There are dry leaves under your feet. Something's moving around in the air. When we're walking on the bridge, my heart stops. The river's below. It's eternal. The sky's up above. It's fucking eternal!

Alla So what? SO WHAT? What about it? What do you want? Do you want to become the river? Or the sky?

Vlad That's what I want. I want to become everything. The river and the sky and loads of other things. Because everyone will find a way to survive without our company. But without rivers – we're fucked. And without the sky – we're also fucked.

Alla Well, fuck. Fucking fuck. So what now – you're going to look for "sky" courses. "How to become a river in one week"?

Vlad No. I've come up with something much cooler than that. Basically, I won't go anywhere with you now. I'll turn off the phone. Easy.

Alla I knew it. Vlad, tell me one thing, as a dumb-girl, why does the search for oneself always start with idleness and getting hammered?

Vlad I'm not going to get pissed. I'm going to search.

Alla Search for what?

Vlad I'll just walk around. I'll look at how people live. But I promise...

Alla I see, but can't I come with you?

Vlad It's not worth it.

Alla I'm already wondering ...

Vlad I want to think. It can't be that everything was created just so we can earn money. Money – I'm afraid, somehow doesn't push towards the next level of evolution.

Alla Okay, fine. I'm going to the café. To see Zhanka. She's in Free Letters now, meeting people on-line. She's really wicked. You know, she found someone there a while back, an Armenian or an Indian or something... with long hair and she said – if he's got long hair, he's got a long dick because all men with long hair are lazy and do nothing but fuck. And that makes men's dicks grow. And he sent her a photo...

Vlad Okay. Good luck. But if I see that there's bollocks everywhere, really everywhere ... and people actually *don't* need anything else – then I'll join you.

Alla Okay. Have a good walk. Just take care, don't get involved in anything bad! Will you walk me there...

Vlad Huh? Yeah, of course, obviously...

Alla Don't worry. I'll go by myself. When will you find your man, Diogenes? I'm asking so I should know when to come back. Or I'll come back to this philosophy again. I wouldn't be able to stand it a second time.

Vlad I'll call you.

Alla Well, okay. Good luck!

At the same time in a different place, a taxi driver is drinking coffee in a small canteen, standing by a table with two other taxi drivers. Not far from them stands a girl, she's watching him. The lighting is dim. There's a smell of cream-in-dough cakes and meat which isn't fresh. People in worn-out leather jackets and cheap coats push and shove all the people mentioned above and each other. Behind the window, blindingly bright white snow falls onto the dirt and dies, as if not able to wait for mother-winter. It would be pointless to shout. That's why everyone talks in half-whispers.

Taxi Driver 1 The weather's bollocks today...

Taxi Driver 2 Today's some kind of "super Sunday"... I heard it on the radio...

Taxi Driver 3 Today's Monday, actually. Sunday? What the fuck's that all about?

Taxi Driver 1 Don't argue, Sasha. Don't argue. They said it on the radio, it's a super Sunday... so it's a super Sunday. The radio knows best.

Taxi Driver 2 Yeah, like fuck they know... they said yesterday, "It's five o'clock", I looked at my watch... I've got seven to. They know... why would they give a fuck – five, seven... they're talking shit the whole journey. So they don't give a toss that people leave early from work.

Taxi Driver 3 And I s'pose you give a toss? Are you the frigging President? Sod all that – Lyosha fucked off seven minutes early in his cab...

Taxi Driver 1 If the President fucks off early – then everything's fucking fantastic... Yeltsin fucked off and everything got a fuck of a lot better... now this one should also piss off somewhere...

Taxi Driver 2 That's what I'm saying!... my brother-in-law works at the car factory now – everything depends on time-keeping. It fucking runs their whole lives. They take away all their watches – because then there's no fucking way of knowing when their shift ends.

Taxi Driver 3 And when did it end?

Taxi Driver 2 Earlier – fuck only knows. At three, now.

Taxi Driver 1 No, I get it at the factory. People have to work, there. But you're just wanking behind the wheel all day – why the fuck do you need to know the time?

Taxi Driver 2 I like everything to be exact. That's the kind of person I am. I'm logical, I need to know what's what.

Girl Are you drivers?

Taxi Driver 3 Where do you need to go?

Girl Home, to Profsoyznaya district.

Taxi Driver 1 On Garibaldi Street?

Girl Right next to it. In New Cheryomiskhi.

Taxi Driver 2 Sasha, will you take her?

Taxi Driver 3 Fuck knows . . . it's like an hour to get there at this time of the . . . (*to the girl*) How much are you paying?

Girl A hundred and fifty.

Taxi Driver 1 That's not a fucking price . . . take the metro.

Girl How much then?

Taxi Driver 2 Two hundred. No less . . .

Taxi Driver 3 Lyosha, fucking hell! Two hundred? Fuck! Even three hundred's not enough, fu-uck . . .

Girl I don't have three hundred . . .

Taxi Driver 1 Then hang around. If someone else needs a taxi, I'll take both of you. If no one else shows up, you're fucked.

Taxi Driver 2 Sasha's wife beats him when he gets home late.

Taxi Driver 3 Fuck off!

Taxi Driver 1 Ah, that's why he needs to know the time! Well, well, tell us about it, Sasha . . .

Taxi Driver 2 She gives him hell, he told me so himself – and you're going on about the President!

Taxi Driver 3 The President also gets beaten by his wife. Have you seen his wife?

Taxi Driver 1 Why does she have to beat him?

Taxi Driver 2 With a face like that, she won't just give him a beating, she'll make him start a war . . .

Taxi Driver 3 That's what he did. All wars start because of women. I read it in a book – a man's alright by himself, but as soon as he marries – he starts sticking his chest out. 'Cos his wife starts grating on him. She'll keep on grating – even if she's not actually *saying* anything.

Taxi Driver 1 They just stare at you like (*he demonstrates*). It's the end!

Taxi Driver 2 It's like the war in Chechnya.

Taxi Driver 3 Same thing in Chechnya. Basaev's woman wakes up one morning, "you're not hard like a real man, you're like a fucking dish towel!" So he goes off and starts blowing up trains.

Taxi Driver 1 Basaev was killed ages ago.

Taxi Driver 2 Yeah, right. Killed. They didn't kill him. He has too much money to be killed. . .

Taxi Driver 3 They'll kill someone with money even quicker.

Taxi Driver 1 Yes, lads, let's drink to Vitya. Today's he's . . . already four days in the ground.

The taxi drivers drink their coffee. At the same time, the girl goes into the canteen toilet. There's only one toilet with unpainted, scratched wooden panels on both sides of it. Opposite is a sink with the bottom beaten out of it, a bit of a mirror stuck to the wall with some sticky tape. A woman with a bag has sat down on the toilet. The girl goes over to her. She takes a syringe out of her bag.

Girl If I jab you with this – you're fucked. I've got AIDS. If you scream for help, I'll be put in jail, but I don't give a fuck. Give me your bag.

The woman hands over her bag. The girl pulls out the wallet, puts it in her pocket, and hits the woman over the head with the bag. An inhaler falls out of the bag. The woman breathes in, deep panicking breaths, a few times. Taxi Driver 3 walks into the toilet. The girl sits down on the woman's knees and kisses the struggling woman on the lips, smearing lipstick all over her and her face. The woman struggles much more weakly now. She jerks a couple of times . . .

Girl (*to Taxi Driver 3*) Are we going, then? To Cheryomushki? Three hundred then, you wanker, just first I need to go to one other place. I'll get out of the car. Then I'll get back in.

Taxi Driver 3 Fuck me . . . the women are at it . . . well, let's go then, you wanker. You'll leave your bag as a guarantee, when you get out.

Taxi Driver 3 washes his hands, turning on the tap carefully so that no water trickles down through the hole in the sink.

Taxi Driver 3 Well, are we going?

Girl Let's go.

Taxi Driver 3 and the girl leave. The woman looks for her inhaler on the floor, in a panic, but her hand is shaking so feverishly that she hits and breaks the inhaler. She continues to sit on the toilet, breathing heavily for some time, and then somebody comes into the toilet and leaves again, hardly looking at her.

Taxi Driver 1 And what was it on the radio about the super Sunday that you was talking about?

Taxi Driver 2 Don't you know how that works? You have to ring up and guess some stupid shit. They squeeze money out of people, there's no chance of winning . . . and you become fucking moronic, waiting to get through. Come on, drink up and let's go and fix this shelf. I won't be able to put it up by myself.

III. WE DON'T HAVE ANYTHING – OUR WHOLE LIVES

Vlad is outside. A huge number of people are walking past him.

Alena Oh, hi! What are you doing?

Vlad Hi. I'm just standing here, watching . . .

Alena You're lucky . . . I can't just stand around . . . I'm coming from work now, my boss is a complete fuck, he's sent me to some guy, secret packet, some info or something, got to give it to him, straight into his hands . . . why didn't he come over himself? He's got a car and fucking everything else, and my car's being fixed, now I've got to get rattled around on the metro . . .

Vlad Why don't you take a taxi?

Alena I wanted to but the traffic . . .

A beggar walks up to them, they're worn-out, dull-looking and weak.

Vlad Sorry, brother. I don't have any money. I said no, go away.

Alena Oh, Alya! Hi!

Alya How are you?

Vlad Fine. Where are you going?

Alya I've got to run. Bye, I'm late for a meeting . . . I've been promised ama-azing sex – fucking brilliant . . . I'll tell you later. Bye-bye, Alena!

Alena Shit. Some people are lucky. Vlad, do you know that discussing sex lowers the rate of productivity?

Vlad But do you know how many people haven't fucked a single time in their lives?

Alena You mean monks?

A goth walks up to them.

Alena Leave us alone, we haven't got money! Go away!

Vlad Are people interested in anything other than money?

Alena Well, there aren't many people like that here – people interested in other things.

Vlad Where are they?

Alena I'm not even sure . . . In the library? No, it's shit there, nothing but poverty . . .

Vlad Academics?

Alena Academics? . . . they're only students. I just wonder why they can't write Russian properly if they're reading so many books? Not long ago, one had written a job application, "I injoy studying". The person gets a job as a manager . . . anyway, have fun, I've got to run . . .

A policeman comes up to Vlad.

Policeman Good evening. Sergeant Malishev. Can I check your registration?

Vlad Of course. What's the matter?

Policeman Nothing yet . . . fine, that's all, thank you, sorry.

The policeman walks off and beats a sitting cripple in the stomach. The cripple wakes up and pulls out some money from under some rags. The policeman takes it and walks away.

A person comes over to Vlad and asks for a cigarette. Vlad gives it to him. The person pulls out a knife and puts it to Vlad's side.

Man Give me your money. Quiet, mate, don't make a fuss.

Policeman What's up?

Man We're just having a chat – I'll come back and see you later! (*He leaves.*)

Policeman Was he giving you trouble?

Vlad Yeah. He wanted to rob me. Just now. He had a knife.

Policeman Will you write a statement? Just do it quickly and I can catch him now, before he's gone too far.

Vlad No, I won't.

Policeman Well, fuck him then. You're wrong, mister. I would have caught him and now he's off finding someone else to rob . . .

Vlad Do you have a wife?

Policeman What's my wife got to do with it?

Vlad Well, where is she now? Maybe he's robbing her?

Policeman Let me have another look at your registration.

Vlad I was just joking.

Policeman Come on, show me your papers. A fucking joker . . .
you want to spend some time in the monkey-house?

Vlad Why in the monkey-house? You're crazy, Sergeant What's-
your-name? I've only just almost been robbed, yes?

Policeman But you refused to write a report? Well that's it, then.
We can only catch him if you write a report. But we can detain *you*
just like that. To find out if you're guilty.

Vlad Well, fine, enough, Sergeant! I apologise.

Policeman An apology is an admission of guilt. So you admit that
you offended a representative of the authorities on duty?

Vlad What the, do you want money, or what?

Policeman Not money . . . a fine. So come on – are we paying up,
or shall I call the boys?

Vlad How much?

Policeman Five hundred roubles – put it in here, in your passport.
And let's step over there, to one side . . .

*The policeman takes the money from his passport and returns the
papers to Vlad, then he leaves.*

A woman comes over to Vlad.

Woman Help me . . . please, help me . . .

Vlad What happened?

Woman I've just been beaten up . . . just now. Not far from here. I
was attacked on the toilet. Help me, if you can . . . it's true. I'm not
a beggar, I'm sorry . . . if you can, give me twenty roubles for a bus
home, I'll go home and I'll give it back to you . . .

Vlad Shit, you're all the same asking for fucking money!

The woman steps back.

Vlad Fuck, do you need anything, apart from money?! You've
got so many opportunities, so much around you, but you don't
give a fuck about any of that! You're sitting in shit, you fucking

stink of piss, and, you bitch, you're asking for money! Go and wash yourself and everything will get better, start with the simple things, and you'll have everything you want!

Woman   Sorry . . . I'm sorry . . . I'm telling you, some girl, right in the toilet, took my wallet and I wanted to . . . but she had a syringe, and she said she had AIDS . . .

Vlad   What the fuck are you talking about! Here's fifty roubles, go and have a fucking vodka, piss yourself again, if you want it that much, go on!

Woman   (*picking up the fifty roubles*) Thank you, young man. I'm not a beggar, I'm really not . . . but when someone came in, a man came in, she sat on me, I was scared, and she started kissing me, but you can't get AIDS from that, can you?

Vlad leaves quickly. And the woman leaves. At the same time, a bloke opens the door and lets another bloke into his flat.

Bloke 1   Well? Is everything alright?

Bloke 2   Yes, everything's fine. Look, are you sure?

Bloke 1   What?

Bloke 2   Why do you need to do this?

Bloke 1   You wouldn't understand.

Bloke 2   Exactly. But this is business. So explain it to me. In a way I can understand, as well.

Bloke 1   Fine. You don't mind if I shoot up at the same time?

Bloke 2   Go ahead. But with full details. Because I reckon there's some philosophy behind this.

Bloke 1 begins to prepare a dose.

Bloke 1   What have you got against philosophy?

Bloke 2   Shit, I mean it's all Jewish crap, isn't it. It's all "there's nothing you can do about it". I don't like that. I don't have time for bollocks like that.

Bloke 1 Okay. It's a stupid story. It's time for me to do something real. That's the short version . . .

Bloke 2 And? Is that all?

Bloke 1 Mm-hm.

Bloke 2 How'd you realise that?

Bloke 1 I always wanted to.

Bloke 2 Well, we all want to do stuff. My dad spent his whole life on his arse, he wanted a lot of things – but he became an alcoholic from wanting.

Bloke 1 I almost became an alcoholic. I read a lot . . . it's bollocks.

Bloke 2 What's bollocks?

Bloke 1 The way I see it, I thought I could save myself through my intellect. Like if you become clever, you understand things. I thought people drink because they don't see things could be better. But books talk about things that are better. Right?

Bloke 2 Fuck knows. I also got hold of something to read – it was some sort of . . . about a gang . . . It put me to sleep, it was shit, basically. I don't read.

Bloke 1 Well, I was reading other books . . . but it doesn't matter. I'm reading and I'm getting worse, all the fucking time. Like the joke about the elk. And then I look around me, and it's exactly the same. It's fucked up.

Bloke 2 What's fucked up?

Bloke 1 Writers also can't do anything. They just describe. Same thing –or they write how they wish things would be. But how can they write about that if they can only imagine how things should be, and even then they spend their whole time doubting it?

Bloke 2 So then what?

Bloke 1 I got fed up. Everyone's fucking reading. We're all going to get fucked up from reading. And anyone who isn't reading is watching. It's fucked . . .

Bloke 2 What's fucked?

Bloke 1   Basically, it's all theory everywhere. It's time to turn on reality. Right. I've said enough.

Bloke 2   Well, I can't really tell you anything about theory – but there are too many bullshitters in reality. Luckily, most of them are in jail.

Bloke 1   Everyone is a bullshitter. Do you see that no-one's doing anything. Everyone is only bullshitting. That's what's so ridiculous.

Bloke 2   There's nothing ridiculous about it. Do you get it? This is a serious business. Robbery. Do you get it? If they catch us, they'll give you, 'cos it's your first time, three years. Do you get it? And then fuck knows where you'll get work. Do you get it?

Bloke 1   Fuck, you can't change my mind like that. No-one's hired me for three years anyway.

Bloke 2   The main thing is – no more philosophy. There was one bloke who said "I won't take someone who's just doing it for kicks. I'll only take someone who's dying of hunger – because then they work properly. Then they'll go as far as they have to, stand up to whatever." That's why I'm having doubts.

Bloke 1   Everything's cool. And you . . . what was your first time?

Bloke 2   What about me?

Bloke 1   Were you also dying of hunger the first time? Or did you just go out of curiosity, because you wanted to watch?

Bloke 2   I wasn't dying of hunger, nah. First time, I . . . well, yeah, out of curiosity, because . . . well, yeah. Shit, that's just philosophy again . . .

Bloke 1   Why are you making a big deal of it? Everything's fine, everything's wicked. If you think I'm going to bottle it – then (*he shows him a knife*).

Bloke 2   Fuck!

Bloke 1   What?

Bloke 2   Are you screwed in the head? Throw it away for fuck's sake . . . just hang a sign on yourself "I'm going to fucking rob someone and cut them up"! Shit.

Bloke 1 But what if . . . well, things don't go as planned?

Bloke 2 That's what I'm saying – that's just philosophy. What won't go as planned? You go in, there's a woman . . .

Bloke 1 And what if there's not just a woman? What if someone else comes in?

Bloke 2 What the fuck? First, nobody else will come. Because no-one ever goes to see old women. Nobody has any fucking need for them. Their relatives only call on them – to check if they're alive or dead, then they can sell the fucking flat, and that's that. And second, you'll get a knife *there*, you'll get everything there anyway. There's everything in the flat. And you almost never need one anyway. They're afraid for their lives. She'll give us everything herself.

Bloke 1 Fine.

Bloke 1 injects himself with heroine. He chuckles.

Bloke 2 What're you smilin' about – what, you just invent a new theory of relativity?

Bloke 1 No . . . aaaah, shit . . . fuck me . . . I just remembered . . . today with Yulia, we were getting into each other in the entrance of the building, I said some good shit about freedom . . .

Bloke 2 What'd you say?

Bloke 1 I said: you're freedom. That's all. You and nothing else.

Bloke 2 Fucking philosophy, again . . .

Bloke 1 Nah . . . I asked her to blow me . . .

Bloke 2 Did she?

Bloke 1 Nah . . .

Bloke 2 Fucking cunt . . . she should be pleased, soon she'll be burned out and no-one's going to offer . . .

Bloke 1 Right. Let's go, yeah?

Bloke 2 Okay. Now – you've got nothing else with you? I dunno, spray can, gun . . .

Bloke 1 Shit, if I had a gun, I wouldn't be sitting here with you. I'd go straight off to Siberia.

Bloke 2 What the fuck are you going to do with a gun in Siberia?

Bloke 1 Fighting with the guerrillas. I'm only going with you because I don't have any money. I need money to leave.

Bloke 2 Fuck – what sort of an accomplice has God sent me. Fuck me. A guerrilla-philosopher...

Bloke 1 What did you think...

Bloke 2 Right, enough talk. Let's go. Or all the old women will be dead and the relatives will have come to share out their inheritance. Let's go...

They leave.

IV. BY THE RIVER

Vlad goes over to the river bank. A man is sitting there, watching his boat.

Vlad Hi. How's things?

Boatman Yes, fine ... how's things? Fine...

Vlad How much for a trip?

Boatman No can do. I'm waiting.

Vlad Who are you waiting for?

Boatman What the fuck's it to you, friend?

Vlad No need to be rude.

Boatman I'm not being rude, I'm just asking.

Pause.

Vlad Can I ask you a question?

Boatman Maybe you'll go fuck yourself?

Vlad Meaning?

Pause.

Vlad No, but, what I'm wondering is . . .

Boatman I don't give a fuck what you're wondering.

Pause.

Boatman Fucking pederasts . . .

Vlad Who?

Boatman What the fuck do you care?

Pause.

Vlad Should I leave?

Boatman I don't give a fuck. Fuck off, if you like. Sit down, if you like.

Vlad I can see you don't give a fuck about anything.

Boatman Too fucking right.

Pause.

Pause.

Pause.

Vlad Are you always this way with people? I mean, do you mind me asking? It's just, there's something I really need to know. And I think you're exactly the right person to tell me. So tell me . . .

Boatman Tell you what?

Vlad Are we all here just to live . . . or is there more than that?

Boatman Are you fucked in the head?

Vlad Why?

Boatman Because you're fucked, as far as I can tell.

Pause.

Vlad I really need to know.

Pause.

Boatman Pederasts, fuck –

Vlad Do you understand, I'm not just asking. I really want to know. I have everything. Everything in my life is fine. I work, I live within my means, I don't owe anyone anything . . . but is that really the main thing? What *is* the main thing? What's the main thing for you? To sit here like this? But for what?

Pause.

Vlad A cop just got money off me for nothing.

Pause.

Vlad I have a girlfriend.

Pause.

Vlad I've always wanted a motorbike. But I'm scared. I might have an accident, and maybe not even a fatal one. And I still want to do a lot of things.

Pause.

Vlad I've got my own flat. And I'm not even thirty yet. The flat's completely mine. For ever.

Pause.

Vlad Sometimes I wake up at night and I feel like I'm not at home. Like someone is about to come in and start dragging me off somewhere. For some reason always to the potato field. But there's nothing there, they dug up all the potatoes already there are people around me, and something starts aching in the back of my head . . . I'm hit by lightening and the people start singing. But a tree grows out of me. Instead of me. And I will never leave this field.

Pause.

Vlad Sometimes in the night, I lift up my head and I can't recognise the place. No, the flat's mine, I understand that, but I think that someone else put everything here while I was away. A table, a bed, shelves, books . . . And you begin to understand that there's someone who will decide everything for you. Who decides absolutely everything. When you'll meet a girl, which one . . . when you leave the house, where you go. And when I die – it's also not me who decides.

Pause.

Boatman Fucking shit.

Vlad What?

Boatman You fucking shit.

Vlad looks at the river with him. Snow clouds gather above the river. Crows begin to crow – they're cold. The ice noiselessly throws itself at the riverbank and remains there forever. The boatman smokes. The wind shoves around the dead plants. Only a cigarette butt hurries past Vlad and the boatman – and nothing else. Vlad lifts up the collar of his coat. At the same time, a girl calls on her mobile phone, standing in front of the door to a flat. A lad comes out of it and sells her heroine. She sits down and prepares it in the lid of a water bottle.

Seller Shit, come on, hurry up! That's enough, come on, let's get this shit over with. The cops come round to mine sometimes. There's someone living up there.

Girl What – you got a problem with them?

Seller What problem with the cops? My problem is with you . . . turn the needle round, shit, you'll fuck it up now . . . give it here, I'll do it . . . you're such an amateur . . .

Girl Stop talking. You're making money from us.

Seller Fuck me . . . and now you think I'm gonna kiss your cunt? I'm making money. You must also be making money. You turned up here, didn't you? Haven't you got anything else to spend money on?

Girl I do what I want. Fuck off.

Seller Shit, if you become President, then you can do what you want!

Girl I am President, as it is. Of myself.

Seller Fuck . . . come on, shoot up, president, and get out of here.

Girl I'm getting there. (*She lifts her trouser leg, rubs her leg, winces from the pain, then, remembering something, lowers her trouser leg.*) I'm getting there. Wait.

The girl lifts her sleeve, closes her eyes and sits unmoving.

Seller Shit, what are you doing, yoga or something?

Girl Quiet. Don't bother me, alright? I need to concentrate.

Seller You a mathematician, or something? Shit, look, come on, sod off down a floor and there you can sing, dance, I don't fucking care, meditate, sit...

Girl Bollocks... you're fucking me off... have you heard about freedom?

Seller You a hippy? Hello, little girl, wake up – the only thing left from the sixties is music. On crappy tapes. Fuck me, shooting up but she sits on the landing having a go at me about freedom. Fucking Nelson Mandela...

Girl Shut it, go away, GO AWAY!

The seller closes the door. The girl sits and stretches out her hand in front of her, with the sleeve of her jacket rolled up. She closes her eyes. The snow falls so slowly beyond the window that you can count the number of snowflakes – but then again who's going to count them? How many people are there who still fly in their dreams? You look at the news and you get the impression: almost nobody. Two people come upstairs, the girl is silent and her eyes are shut – in the windows there's nobody but sky and nobody even throws rubbish out because everyone is so afraid to go outside. Two men crouch down right in front of the girl. It seems pretty clear that our planet is very big – big enough, either the landing is too small or there are too many stairs in it and all the walls are rushing somewhere (though it's not clear where) – up or down. The walls couldn't give a damn. The girl opens her eyes and wants to inject herself with the syringe but she sees the people.

They take her by the arms and put her face to the wall. They take her jeans and pants off. She thinks they are going to fuck her but they lift up her arm twisted behind her back and she bends down

lower, even lower, until her head is practically touching the floor.
Then they kick her sexual organs. Then they will force her to lick
their boots. Then they will force her to lie on the floor, in the dirt and
blood, and the sun would glance into her eyes but they're shut and at
the same time they will piss on her and then make her kneel again.
They will kick her forehead with their boots. Her head will hit the
wall, and the syringe will fall out of her hands and bounce down the
stairs. Someone will put on a condom and force her to suck his dick.
While that's happening, she won't be thinking of anything. She will
just dully suck the latex-covered dick, give in and not think. But her
forehead will be throbbing and the joints of her arms will be hurting.
It's quiet on the landing, anyone who normally goes somewhere
won't go anywhere now – they're not idiots, are they? And not one
pensioner will stand up for her. And she will understand that all of
her freedom is herself. Then he will take his dick out of her mouth,
wipe it on her face (in fact, he's wiping the sperm off on her), then
they'll leave. Then she picks up the syringe, leaves the building and
gets back into the taxi.

Girl Let's go.

Taxi Driver What happened to your face? Your bloke, was it?

Girl My bloke, my bloke. Come on, let's go.

Taxi Driver You have to choose your bloke carefully. There are
hardly any normal ones nowadays. They've forced Russia to drink
– everyone drinks, and then, shit, obviously, you get a beating. You
can't beat the President up, fuck even knows where he is . . . And
you won't beat yourself up – because that would mean saying it as
it is, no? Admitting you were wrong . . . we can't do that, of course
. . . Well it's too painful, obviously . . . Though – pretty easy. Do
you want a tissue? No? It's the whole government of course. Send
the whole fucking lot of them to Chechnya, the ones that drink
– easy as that, I reckon. Give them a carriage full of vodka each.
Either they'll get wasted and fuck up all the Chechens, or they'll
fall asleep and then the Chechens would slice them all up. That
would be much better for Russia. In any case . . .

The girl looks out of the window. There are grey streets and houses,
full of people. The bright shop windows light up her face. People

*aren't reflected in them, which makes it seem as if there are no
people. And the darkness reflects. Goods loom out of the darkness
like traps. The girl itches her wrist. She takes the syringe out of her
pocket and looks at it for some time, then, not looking, injects herself
in the wrist, making it seem as if she's adjusting her trouser-leg.*

V. OUR BUSINESS

The blokes sit on a tree opposite the selected window.

Bloke 1 So who's first?

Bloke 2 Me of course.

Bloke 1 Why you?

Bloke 2 You won't be quick enough. But we gotta be quick. It's
hardest for the first person – he's got to scare the crap out of her.

Bloke 1 And how are you going to scare her?

Bloke 2 Beat her up a bit, that's all. A little bit.

Bloke 1 And will she get scared?

Bloke 2 Why the fuck wouldn't she get scared? She'll think I'm
going to fucking kill her.

Bloke 1 We're not going kill her then?

Bloke 2 Shit, why the fuck would we kill her? Has she done
anything to you?

Bloke 1 No.

Bloke 2 Well, then, what the fuck? If she was a pig, that'd be
different. . .

Bloke 1 She wasn't, yeah?

Bloke 2 No.

Bloke 1 What was she?

Bloke 2 I fucking know?

Bloke 1 How do you know she isn't a pig, then?

Bloke 2 Pigs are different.

Bloke 1 What way?

Bloke 2 Fuck knows . . . just different. They behave differently. Everything about them is different. There she is, can you see her? Oh, shit, what a cunt . . .

Bloke 1 Can't she see us?

Bloke 2 She can't see a fucking thing. When I came before, I was watching her, it took her three times to find her letter box.

Bloke 1 Cool . . .

Bloke 2 Maybe not so cool . . . Means she might not have anything . . . though they gave out their pensions today, I checked. Right, come on, I'll climb in, so basically, as soon as I open the window – straight in after me. Understood?

Bloke 1 Understood. Don't we need to cover our faces?

Bloke 2 Why would we cover our faces?

Bloke 1 Well, so she doesn't recognise us. They always do that in the films.

Bloke 2 Has she seen you before or something?

Bloke 1 No, 'course not . . .

Bloke 2 Then how's she gonna recognise you?

Bloke 1 Well, but, later, when the cops come, she'll describe us . . .

Bloke 2 Shit, where've you been hanging out all this time? Fuck . . . describe us? Right, describe me now, just do it quickly.

Bloke 1 Well, fuck knows . . . you're . . . wide face . . . normal, ordinary nose, blue eyes. Dark hair. Cheek bones . . .

Bloke 2 Cheek bones fucking shmeek bones . . . do you understand what you came up with? You won't get a single fucker with what you just described.

Bloke 1 How do the cops do it, then?

Bloke 2 Same as always. They find a pair of druggies, beat 'em up, they own up and they blame it on them. You're a druggie, but you think like a cunt, like a fucking school boy . . .

Bloke 1 Fine, fine, I'm an idiot, let's just climb in quickly before the whole building knows we're here . . .

Bloke 2 They don't give a fuck – we're not robbing *them*, are we? Right, I'm climbing in now, okay. Right after me. *Right* after me. Don't hang around in the window.

Bloke 1 Wicked, let's go.

They climb through the window. Hanging on the wall of this old flat, which hasn't been renovated for a long time, is a calendar with a smiling Gagarin in a red helmet with a huge bouquet of flowers. The side-board, the big dining table, several chairs, the bed-side table with a television on it, the wardrobe, the sofa, the coffee table, and the armchair are all standing so close to each other that you need to walk sideways to squeeze past them. The television is very cheap and small.

Bloke 2 (*shouting at the old woman*) Give us your money! Give us your money! Everything you got! Everything you got! Come on, bitch, give it over! Quickly! (*To Bloke 1*) Shit! Shut the window, for fuck's sake!

Bloke 1 shuts the window, roots around the wardrobe, looking in the shelves, throws everything on the floor, stamps on them, rips the tablecloth from the table, letting the vase fall to the floor, and the old woman's papers are underneath it. Bloke 1 takes the vase and throws it against the wall.

Bloke 1 I'm going to fuck this place apart! Where, bitch, where is everything? Come on, bitch, I'm going to fuck this place apart! (*He takes her papers and looks at them.*) Valentina Mikhailovna? You're in the fuck now, Valentina Mikhailovna . . .

Bloke 2 What the fuck are you looking at, you fucking lamb? Give us your money!

Valentina Mikhailovna There . . . it's there. There . . . in the table, in the drawer there . . . in that secretaire . . .

Bloke 1 The secretaire? That drawer? (*He pulls it open, throws everything out of it, he finds the money under a newspaper.*) Is that everything?

Bloke 2 Give us more! Give us more, bitch! Where's your bag?! Where's your purse?!

Valentina Mikhailovna The bag's there . . . in the hall . . . I went to the shop . . . to the shop, it's still in the hall . . . don't kill me, please, just don't touch me, I'm ill . . .

Bloke 2 goes into the hall for the bag.

Bloke 1 (*shouts after him*) Look, she has a cutlery set, shit . . . it's silver . . . do we take that?

Bloke 2 (*from the hall*) Take everything!

Bloke 1 pours the contents of the drawer into a plastic bag. He goes over to the cupboard. He sees a blouse on a hanger with a medal on its lapel.

Bloke 1 Fuck me . . . are you a veteran? You a fucking veteraness? (*He reads the medal.*) For building . . . did you build communism? No poor, no rich? Turned out fucking great for you, yes? It's all wicked for you? Now you sit around getting high on your two thousand, yes?

Bloke 2 Right, fuck, she hasn't got a fucking thing. Let's beat it.

Bloke 1 Right, come on, come on!

Bloke 2 (*to Valentina Mikhailova*) You. Are. A. Cunt. Sit here quietly. Or you're fucked. If you jump up to call the cops – I'll fuck you up. Not me, the others. Got it?

Bloke 1 Bitch you won't live to see your fucking communism, you cunt, you got that?

Valentina Mikhailovna I won't, I won't, lads, good lads, I won't, I won't . . .

Blokes 1 and 2 leave. Valentina Mikhailova's hands and lips are trembling. She sits still. Snow drifts in through the open window. Dirty traces are left on the window sill. The rest of the tablecloth slips silently to the floor. At the same time, Vlad is in a taxi. The radio's on, there's broken glass. From time to time, the heater turns itself on. On the seat next to the driver sits a girl, indifferently staring at one spot.

Taxi Driver Are you going to relatives?

Vlad No. I'm just exploring. I want to remember my childhood. I grew up there, I just want to see it. What it's like, how much things have changed . . .

Taxi Driver Everything's changed now.

Vlad Well, the same trees are standing . . .

Taxi Driver If they haven't cut them down, they're still standing . . .

Vlad When I get out I'll buy some vodka and I'll go to the playground and sit on a roundabout, get on a fairground ride, take a ride. It'll be good. Then I'll go into a stairwell – and I'll drink. When I was a lad, they always chased us away from stairwells . . . but they won't chase me away now. It's cool.

Taxi Driver Everything's fucking great, if you don't need to do a fucking thing.

Vlad You know, you're like someone . . . just now I . . . On the river bank, before I got in your car, I was sitting with someone. Him, too – either silent or swearing. Why is that do you think?

Taxi Driver Everyone has their own reasons.

Vlad And you?

Taxi Driver For me, there's no reason. Actually, I envy you. What do you do?

Vlad Oh, you know . . . I'm a manager in an office.

Taxi Driver And what do you do?

Vlad Finance. Mainly analysis. Do you know about Macklersky's broker analysis?

Taxi Driver No.

Vlad Then you won't understand.

Taxi Driver I couldn't give a fuck. How much do you get a month?

Vlad Around five.

Taxi Driver No fucking way! Dollars?

Vlad Yes.

Taxi Driver Not fucking bad. Then of course you can drive around, drinking vodka, of course...

Vlad Do you think we don't do any damn work?

Taxi Driver Why would I think that? Of course, they don't pay five for nothing, everyone knows that...

Vlad Well, there you go.

Taxi Driver Just – things are easier for you.

Vlad Well, how can I put it? Sometimes you want something... the thing which made you a person before. I mean, we became the way we are because of something magical? No? Am I wrong?

Taxi Driver I'm not even sure how to answer that. Something made us the way we are, probably. We were all younger, we all wasted time on some bollocks or other.

Vlad Like for you, I bet you loved cars as a child, being with your father... your father probably had a car? And you climbed in and took it all apart... or you went to visit him at work? To the garage or in his workshop? No?

Taxi Driver My father worked on a building site. He took me with him, of course. And me and the boys used to climb around the building site at night. I knew exactly what was where, where the linoleum was, where the wallpaper was... we got the keys, I took copies – and we climbed in. We threw things over the fence then sold them to the Georgians. It was alright. And then the Georgians killed my father. Not those ones, others. And we moved to Moscow. My mother said "we should go or you'll end up in jail". So fuck only knows who was thinking what to themselves as children, and then life comes along and fuck. And that's that.

Vlad So there was no magic for you?

Taxi Driver Magic in my childhood? My mother would give me a present for the New Year, you'd ask her where it was from. She's say – Father Christmas, that's the whole fucking thing.

Vlad Listen! . . .

Taxi Driver What?

Vlad Can we change the music?

Taxi Driver Sure. (*He switches off the radio.*)

Pause.

Vlad Hey!

Taxi Driver Yes?

Vlad I didn't say turn it off. I asked if you could change it . . .

Taxi Driver What else is there worth listening to? I don't like anything else . . .

Vlad Actually, I always wanted to ask – what is it about your prison songs?

Taxi Driver Why *my* prison songs?

Vlad Well, for as long as I've been taking taxis, taxi drivers are the only people listening to it, mainly.

Taxi Driver Not true at all. All my friends listen to it. They're not all drivers.

Vlad Right, and who are your friends, actually?

Taxi Driver They're normal blokes . . . just people, just . . .

Vlad And they all listen to prison songs?

Taxi Driver Well, yes . . . what else is there to listen to? Pop music? Do you think we're total idiots?

Vlad But other than pop?

Taxi Driver No, there's rock, but I can't . . . my ears get tired. I've got to go round town all day, can you imagine?

Vlad So?

Taxi Driver So . . . if I've got that shitting in my ears my whole shift, loudly – I can go fucking crazy. So I mustn't.

Vlad So your passenger will suffer instead?

Taxi Driver What has my passenger got to do with it? The passenger can go to hell, for all I care. I could run someone over – and not everyone has the money to go to hospital nowadays.

Vlad And your passenger does?

Taxi Driver Well, they've got in my taxi, so it means they've got money. If you don't have money, you take a bus.

Vlad That's logical.

Taxi Driver Well-yeah . . .

Pause.

Vlad And at home, do you also listen to prison songs?

Taxi Driver Why? Yes, I do. I've already told you – what else is there to listen to? Or are you too . . . too refined, or something? You don't like the truth?

Vlad Are prison songs the truth?

Taxi Driver Why not? Normal guys telling good stories. Who, how, the whole thing . . . Who else will tell you things like that? Putin on the telly? That's the way he looks at life . . .

Vlad What way?

Taxi Driver The way he looks at television! And they'll show it to you there, of course . . . you know when they cut off heating from the pensioners. The pensioners went out onto the square. Were they right to do that?

Vlad Probably . . .

Taxi Driver Why were they right?

Vlad I don't know . . . what do you mean?

Taxi Driver I mean. You're not going to sit there and light a bonfire in your flat? At home you've just redecorated the whole thing . . . it will get blackened by smoke, no?

Vlad So that's why they went onto the square? Not to demonstrate?

Taxi Driver My friend, they haven't demonstrated for a long time. After a demonstration, you've got to smash windows, that's what you do. But which one of them's going to go and smash a window? They're all old, they wouldn't have the strength. You have to shout and swear at a demonstration. It's hard for them to shout and they're embarrassed by swearing.

Vlad So why then?

Taxi Driver They stand, light fires, talk to each other. What – they're not people? Well, the press came to film them. The were girls in boots, in make-up, pouting, looking beautiful, they couldn't give a toss right. Demonstration, protest, all they want is some nice footage to add some pretty words to. They don't give a fuck. They made it look like a provincial social gathering. And Putin – what does he see? He sees what they show him.

Vlad And we started talking about prison songs . . . what are you trying to say?

Taxi Driver Okay, if you take Misha Krug, for example, – he's experienced everything. He's lived everything and hasn't betrayed anybody. He knows life a hundred times better.

Vlad Why do you think that?

Taxi Driver Well, I listen to his songs. A person sings what's inside himself, right? If someone's an idiot, like in our pop music, then they sing accordingly. This way, that way, let's go and fuck each other, let's go and suck each other . . . I'm on the beach, you're out of reach . . .

Vlad People do listen to it, on the other hand. . .

Taxi Driver I only listen to it when I'm drunk. Prison songs . . . what's prison about it, when you look at it? The boy's sitting there, pining for his mother. His woman's betrayed him – he killed her and left, and that's it. And that's all there is to the prison song.

Vlad Well, not everyone finds it pleasant to listen to, do they?

Taxi Driver Is the whole sucking each other thing pleasant? Rots your brains . . . right, seems we've arrived. This building?

The driver stops the car. The girl falls forward and knocks her head on the dashboard.

Pause.

Vlad Is she drunk or something?

Taxi Driver Nah, seems to be a druggie. Got in at Novogireevo – says, take me somewhere . . . couldn't make out where. I don't give a toss, we'll work it out. How to get there. And she sits there, shifting around doing something . . . and then – sweet f.a. Seems, she got high. While we were at the traffic lights, seems like she shot up . . . I told her – get out, but I couldn't get a reaction out of her. She's got no money either. And she isn't speaking.

Vlad (*looking at the girl*) I don't think she's breathing any more, by the way.

Taxi Driver Yes, I can see that myself. I'll take her somewhere now and throw her out. Right, I'm off.

Vlad gets out of the car. The taxi driver picks up the next passenger and leaves.

6. Someone avenges me – Me and nobody else

Hanging on the wall of this old flat, which hasn't been renovated for a long time, is a calendar with a smiling Gagarin in a red helmet with a huge bouquet of flowers. The side-board, the big dining table, several chairs, the bed-side table with a television on it, the wardrobe, the sofa, the coffee table, and the armchair are all standing so close to each other that you need to walk sideways to squeeze past them. The television is very cheap and small.

Valentina Mikhailovna sits at the table and wraps herself in a shawl. A policeman is perching opposite her, on the edge of the table, next to the telephone, writing. It smells of valerian. A draft is coming through the wide-open window and the door, open a crack.

Valentina Mikhailovna And I just sat, my programme was meant to start . . . what's it called . . . sorry, my mind's gone blank, I'll remember it in a moment. . .

Policeman It's not essential.

Valentina Mikhailovna Ah, yes. Ah, yes. Of course, not essential. Of course. Forgive me. Now, I'll go on . . .

Policeman Don't hurry, Valentina . . . (*looks at her papers*).

Valentina Mikhailovna . . . Mikhailovna.

Policeman Mikhailovna. So, you were sitting at home, watching television. What next? Someone climbed through the window, yes?

Valentina Mikhailovna Yes, I'm sitting, here . . . but I'm sitting quietly as usual . . . waiting for my programme . . . and I hear a leg shuffling around there . . .

Policeman A leg shuffling around? You were certain that it was a leg shuffling around?

Valentina Mikhailovna Well, yes . . . I'm on the second floor here . . . and it's not like he flew up here or something?

Policeman Well, true, it's definitely not superman?

Valentina Mikhailovna What?

Policeman No, I just wanted to amuse you. It's not superman, is it? He doesn't have wings, does he?

Valentina Mikhailovna Are you saying that to me seriously?

Policeman I just wanted to calm you down . . .

Valentina Mikhailovna Don't. Don't calm me down. If you catch him, then I'll calm myself down. I'll calm myself down. They grabbed my whole pension – and put a knife here, and I'm a labour veteran incidentally, I built all of this, I . . . I have a medal from the state but they took the medal, they were saying – why do you have this medal, you still haven't swapped it for money, and they were laughing, the bastards . . . excuse me, but I . . .

Policeman Right, fine, fine, fine. We're calm. Drink some valerian drops here . . . please continue.

Valentina Mikhailovna (*sobbing*) Thank you. That's good, thank you. Let me tell you more. I just froze. It was in broad daylight, can you imagine? They just went and climbed up, just like that.

Everyone's at home, and they just went and climbed up . . . and he does that with his hand. And I'm sitting, just s –

Policeman Right. They climbed through the window and opened the lock with one hand, is that it? I'm writing it in the report.

Valentina Mikhailovna Write it down, write it down. And write that he threatened me with death. He came right up but another one was climbing in through the window, just like the other one, and the one who had already climbed in . . .

Policeman (*looking at his watch*) Why aren't they coming? (*He dials.*) Central, this is inspector of division 16. Connect me with "Snowdrop". Say that I called there half an hour ago. Yes, I'm waiting. I'm taking a testimony, it's a clear-cut case, tell them to hurry up. Yes, preferably with a dog. Practically nothing's been moved, so we're hot on their tracks. Bye. (*He puts down the phone.*) They'll be here soon.

Valentina Mikhailovna The main thing is to get back my pension and medal, and the rest you probably won't manage to get back . . .

There's noise by the front door. Someone comes in to the flat.

Voices Grandma! Hi! You haven't called the police yet have you? We forgot one piece of shit . . .

Policeman (*to Valentina Mikhailovna, as quick as a tongue-twister*) Just be quiet! I can't take them without a gun! Let me hide, and you give them what they ask for, right, and that's it, but then we'll grab them all at once and we'll get everything back to you. Just don't say I'm here.

Before Valentina Mikhailovna has time to say anything, the police officer grabs his papers and hides behind the curtain. Two blokes come into the room in sports clothes and leather jackets. Valentina Mikhailovna sobs.

Bloke 1 Hi, grandma!

Valentina Mikhailovna Boys, please, well, leave me in peace . . .

Bloke 2 Sorry, lady, we forgot one piece of shit here.

Bloke 1 Ah, there it is (*he takes the lamp from the table*).

Valentina Mikhailovna I called the police. They'll be here any second. . .

Bloke 2 Cool, I didn't see it straightaway . . . (*to Valentina Mikhailovna*). What? Who did you call? (*He tears out the phone line.*) What? What did you – you whore, you bitch, you called them, did you?

Bloke 1 We told you, didn't we? We asked you nicely like any decent person. No?

Valentina Mikhailovna Oh, boys, I'm sorry. . .

Bloke 2 What do you mean, sorry?! What do you mean sorry, you bitch, eh?! (*He slaps Valentina Mikhailovna across the face.*) Did you fuck up, you cow?!

Valentina Mikhailovna begins to cry silently.

Bloke 1 (*hits Valentina Mikhailovna across the face*) Shall I punch your lights out, cunt?!

Vlad walks into the room.

Vlad Comrades, what are you shouting about, sorry, but. . .?

Bloke 1 Get out of here, mate, got it?! We're dealing with this, okay?

Bloke 2 Brother, what are you doing in someone else's flat, eh? We're talking, we're not shouting, go away. . .

Vlad Hold on, did you call her a cow? Well?

Bloke 2 Why're you interfering brother, why are you getting involved, eh? It's fine, we're sorting this out who's a cow and who everyone is, everything. . .

Vlad What are you doing to her?

Bloke 1 Do you understand, it's none of your fucking business what we're doing here?

Valentina Mikhailovna Help me! Help me!

Bloke 1 You bitch I'm going to fucking do both of you, right now. . .

Vlad grabs the cheap, small television and hits Bloke 2 with it, as hard as he can.

He pulls the tablecloth off the table and covers Bloke 1 with it.

He hits him with the box in which the spoons are kept.

He hits him with the box in which the spoons are kept.

Bloke 2 stands up.

Vlad takes the television which has bounced away and throws it at Bloke 2 again.

He kicks Bloke 2.

Nothing is visible – only blood staining the wallpaper.

It stains the wallpaper.

It stains the wallpaper.

Bloke 1 begins to stand up.

Vlad takes a pencil from the floor and jabs somewhere into the tablecloth.

A howl.

Bloke 2 writhes on the floor.

Vlad goes over to him and takes out the dining table drawer and hits him on the head.

And then he kicks him again.

Bloke 1 finally takes the tablecloth off – it's hanging on the pencil.

Vlad turns to him and hits him again, with the telephone.

The curtain falls which was hiding the policeman.

The policeman doesn't move.

Bloke 2 crawls to the door.

Vlad takes the sewing machine off the coffee table and hits Bloke 2 on the head.

Valentina Mikhailovna squeals.

The policeman doesn't move.

Bloke 1 covers his head with his hands and tries to crawl out off the window.

The policeman suddenly grabs the vase which is about to fall off the windowsill.

Vlad steps with his leg on the tablecloth which has become attached to Bloke 1 and doesn't let him out.

Vlad squeezes his head to the window and beats it with the frame several times.

The vase falls from the window-frame.

Valentina Mikhailovna is not shouting anymore.

All of this is happening several centimetres from the policeman.

The policeman doesn't move.

The glass in the window shatters.

Bloke 1 falls to the ground.

Bloke 2 was on the ground a long time ago, dead.

Vlad (*looks around*) I'm sorry. It's turned out rather messy. I'll help you to tidy up . . . (*he takes the tablecloth, it moves Bloke 1, too, he pulls out the pencil and begins to mop the floor*).

Valentina Mikhailovna sobs.

Valentina Mikhailovna Let me do it myself. Thank you, young man. Let me do it, I'll do it myself. (*She collects the fragments of telephone and television from the floor.*)

Vlad Am I right in thinking, this is the second time they came?

Valentina Mikhailovna Yes. You're right. They were completely mad. They have mothers. They have, everyone has a mother, they have . . .

The medal falls out of Bloke 1's pocket. Valentina Mikhailovna catches it on the floor.

Vlad There it is.

Valentina Mikhailovna Let me . . . thank you. Thank you . . . (*She lifts the lamp and puts it on the bedside table.*) Lord, I'm so glad it didn't break.

Vlad It's beautiful.

Valentina Mikhailovna It's my lucky one. It's – my lucky one. We lived in um . . . in Murmansk, in the war. And mama goes out to work, and we put up the black, they were always flying over bombing us . . . and I shut the window and I got under the bed . . .

Vlad Weren't you afraid?

Valentina Mikhailovna It's now I'm afraid . . . I climbed under the bed and wasn't afraid, and I wanted to read. To read a book. And so I (*she shows him*) hung a cover from the bed to the floor so not a shred of light, nothing . . . and the lamp, this one . . . and it shone brightly under the bed, and I was just afraid that the Germans would see it from their planes, and would fly over and bomb us. And mama would come back from work and they would bomb our house. I was afraid that mama would swear at me, that they would bomb our house. And I fell asleep, then mama came back from work . . . (*she cries*). It's my . . . my lucky one . . .

Vlad and Valentina Mikhailovna tidy up.

Valentina Mikhailovna (*to the policeman*) Stand over here, I'm going to wipe that bit.

The policeman obediently moves.

Policeman I'll go, it's . . . I'll call from the neighbours'. Can I call from theirs?

Valentina Mikhailovna Go.

Policeman (*to Vlad*) You shouldn't . . . don't be afraid. I'll tell them that I did it all. Yes? I'll tell them I did it all, otherwise they'll put you in jail, alright?

Valentina Mikhailovna (*to Vlad*) Let him say that, alright? Thank you so much, young man. From my whole being, I . . . but let him say that. Otherwise, it's true they'll put you in prison. You know yourself what the laws now . . .

Policeman Come on, I'll call now, and you go, don't be afraid. Everything's fine – I'll tell them, they came back, and I only did what I did to them . . . because of the circumstances. I'll say I acted according to the circumstances, and everything will be fine. They won't put me in jail . . . (*looks around*) probably. . .

Vlad Yes. Okay, I'm going. I'm done, I'm leaving. Good bye, all the best to you.

Valentina Mikhailovna Thank you, young man. What's your name?

Vlad Vladimir.

Policeman And your surname?

Valentina Mikhailovna Thank you, Vlad. Thank you. Go, leave us, or else they'll arrest you, it's true.

Vlad Good bye. I mean – that's it, good bye. Alright. I mean, hold on. Sorry . . . I probably haven't quite . . . so you just – live like that, that's all, yes?

Valentina Mikhailovna Like what?

Vlad You just live just like this, that's all. Yes? Well, you were just remembering something . . . and that's all, yes? Sorry. Alright. I'm going.

He leaves. At the same time. The taxi drivers are drinking coffee in a small canteen. There are printed-out jokes from the Internet hanging on the walls, fat black arrows pointing to the exit. Outside the window, everything on earth is trying to be. The houses stand so close to each other . . . they are close, unlike us, unlike everyone else. The houses, and nothing but the houses.

Taxi Driver 3 What about our children? *Will* they be left after us? What are you talking about, think about it . . . !

Taxi Driver 1 So who will be left?

Taxi Driver 2 Shit will be left, that's for sure. . .

Taxi Driver 3 Only shit. But only if it becomes as hard as rock. . .

Taxi Driver 1 And if not? You think it won't be left?

Taxi Driver 2 It will get hard as rock, where the fuck else would it go . . . so for example, where my mother lives, in her courtyard, where no fucker has been for a hundred years, I had a massive dump behind the building when my mother took me there when I was three years old . . .

Taxi Driver 3 Not a fucking thing will be left. Not one fucking thing. Not one.

Taxi Driver 1 Don't be stupid . . . something will be left. Look at you – "only shit"? Shit – that's just a load of crap . . .

Taxi Driver 2 Anyway, it was lying there, I went round to piss, I had some beer, so I went over to see how she was, I drank some more beer – and I go for a piss, and there it is, lying there, and I know, I'm sure, that it's mine, there's no doubt about it . . .

Taxi Driver 3 They fuck, and every other one injects themselves.

Taxi Driver 1 Don't be stupid, "they fuck", and maybe you don't fuck . . .

Taxi Driver 2 I'll tell you who fucks! I pick up on weekends from the clubs – from "Point", and from that other one . . .

Taxi Driver 3 "Propaganda"?

Taxi Driver 1 "Dirty weekend"?

Taxi Driver 2 What fucking "Dirty weekend"?! From that other one . . . from the "Bunker". If you drink like they drink, not one fucker, apart from shit, will be left. And even the shit won't be left. Because they don't even shit, they only piss.

Taxi Driver 3 You think they need to fucking shit – to shit you need to eat, but they only booze and sniff? Am I right, that is where shit comes from?

Taxi Driver 1 Listen, that's enough, alright, huh? I'm eating . . .

Taxi Driver 2 Why'd you start the conversation then?

Taxi Driver 3 Like fuck they fuck – all they fucking do is suck cocks. They sit on the back seat and they're at it . . .

Taxi Driver 1 I was fucking talking about children! About who's going to be left after us! About the new generation, how it's going to grow up – and we're sitting here, and they're already . . . well, fucking, and we're sitting here and doing fuck all!

Taxi Driver 2 Sure they fuck, so what? You envious, or something? Fucking throw him out of the car next time and she'll give you a blow-job, she won't fucking care who she does it to!

Taxi Driver 3 I'll show you what will be left, right now. When we were sitting here, right – do you remember, the girl who got in my car today . . .

Taxi Driver 1 Wait, is it *that* one? Who robbed the woman in the toilet?

Taxi Driver 3 What woman?

Taxi Driver 1 . . . you left, a woman shot out of there, from the toilet – your girl showed her something, a syringe or something, or a needle or whatever, and said she had AIDS.

Taxi Driver 2 Fucking simple as that.

Taxi Driver 3 Then what?

Taxi Driver 1 Then, got all her money – (*he whistles*), can you fucking imagine, and goes off with you. The woman wanted to get find out your cab number but I told her you were nothing to do with it.

Taxi Driver 2 Why don't I know about this? I was here?

Taxi Driver 3 Fuck me . . .

Taxi Driver 1 Don't "fuck me", but you owe me a bottle . . .

Taxi Driver 2 Oh, I did look in – there was a woman, yeah. But she was sitting on the toilet, so I went out, I really needed a piss, and she was just fucking sitting there . . . I went off to piss somewhere else . . .

Taxi Driver 3 You're talking crap, Lyosha. I do owe you a fucking bottle. As it is, I'm driving on a temporary driving license – I don't need any more trouble from the fucking cops . . .

Taxi Driver 1 Good. But I'm Gosha, Sasha.

Taxi Driver 2 Gosha the Terrible!

Taxi drivers 2 and 3 laugh till they cry. Several steps away, if you leave the canteen and walk down the cold, beat-up staircase which smells of shortbread, with little steps of the same officially-ordered size, their cars are parked.

Taxi Driver 3 What can I tell you lads – guess who's sitting in my car right now?

Taxi Driver 2 Fuck! . . . Ivan the Terrible's sitting in your car?!

Taxi Driver 3 Very funny . . . the girl, the girl's sitting in my car.

Taxi Driver 1 The one who robbed the other one?

Taxi Driver 3 Uh-huh.

Taxi Driver 1 Why didn't you say? Let's take her to the fucking cops.

Taxi Driver 2 Look at you, a fucking fascist – to the cops . . .! Has she robbed someone, huh?

Taxi Driver 1 No, but what about that woman, no?

Taxi Driver 2 What if she did! Did she write a statement about it? There's no fucking documentary evidence . . . you'll never fucking prove she's even been in here . . .

Taxi Driver 1 So what are you suggesting?

Taxi Driver 2 Let's fuck her ourselves – we won't give her to anyone, alright. We'll fuck her quietly and drop her off. . .

Taxi Driver 3 She's dead, lads.

Taxi Driver 1 She's dead? Why the fuck did you kill her?

Taxi Driver 2 She didn't pay, or something? I mean, fuck her, but did you need to kill her for that?

Taxi Driver 3 Ah, shit, lads . . .

Taxi Driver 1 You'll end up with no passengers at all . . . fuck . . . think about that!

Taxi Driver 3 Look, it wasn't me! She shot up – why did I even tell you about it . . . shit . . . it was just an example.

Taxi Driver 1 Some fucking example – driving a dead woman round town, fuck!

Taxi Driver 2 It's an example of you being a pervert, as far as I can tell. . .

Taxi Driver 3 I'm not a pervert, I'm normal! Where was I going to put her, for fuck's sake, in the middle of town!

Taxi Driver 1 Could have driven her away and thrown her out in the bushes – let her rot there!

Taxi Driver 2 Exactly, and in the morning a snow plough would find her – fuck, who the fuck would recognise her then . . .

Taxi Driver 3 Oi, what's up with you two today, you're both fucked up, lads. . .

Taxi Driver 1 Main thing is, what the fuck are you going to do with her now?

Taxi Driver 3 I'll take her to the building site in Bibirevo.

Taxi Driver 1 And what about before?

Taxi Driver 3 Fuck before – I've had loads of passengers, you think I'm gonna lose money 'cos of that whore?

Taxi Driver 1 Were you driving round with her all day?

Taxi Driver 2 And you're telling us you're normal?

They laugh. The window in taxi driver 3's car opens slowly. The girl looks outside with surprise and exhaustion. It's still winter out there. She thought that no less than a thousand years had passed. She pushes the door and gets out of the car.

Taxi Driver 3 Shut up!

Taxi Driver 1 Shit . . . you're going to start renting her out, aren't you?

Taxi Driver 2 Fu-uck . . . domestic suction for a rouble. . .

Taxi Driver 3 Get lost – I'll fucking throw her out by myself, I was just giving an example, you were talking about the younger generation growing . . .

Taxi Driver 1 What fucking generation – you had a dead girl in your car all day . . . drove around town . . .

Taxi Driver 2 He says, "I'll throw her out" – ha! I'll just drive her to the zoo first and then . . .

They roar with laughter. The girl breathes for the second time in her life, walks, holding on to the wall, she takes the handrail, and steps onto the stairs with pleasure. The winter hides in the darkness. Only cold and quiet remain. These are dead, the ones she was just playing with in the moon's light, crossed by the light from the stars, they watch her with envy. All the traffic lights on the street turn to green. The birds set off somewhere, imagining that they gather together in a flock.

Taxi Driver 3 I'm fucking unhappy with you gentlemen. You're not serious, shit.

Taxi Driver 2 You're fucking serious, though – perhaps suddenly the girl suits you, like . . .

Taxi Driver 1 (*imitating an Estonian accent*) Shee no suitz me! . . .

They are exhausted from laughing. Vlad overtakes the girl on the stairs. He wants to go to the toilet. Not looking at the drivers laughing at their table, Vlad disappears through the door of the toilet.

Taxi Driver 3 (*looking towards Vlad*) Shit, that's the bloke who was in my cab today . . .

Taxi Driver 1 (*sharply turning but not seeing anything – Vlad has already gone into the toilet*) Is he also dead? Where is he?

Taxi Driver 2 Gone round town picking up stiffs. Sasha . . . it's too much!

Taxi Driver 1 Un-huh, and drove around . . .

They laugh. The girl goes past them. Taxi driver 3 goggles at her, the two other taxi drivers look at him and roar. Taxi driver 3 shrugs helplessly and laughs with them. The girl goes into the toilet. She washes, being careful with the water and the sink. She gets the syringe out of her pocket, looks at it and – with a sharp movement – opens the door of the only cabin. Vlad looks at her.

Girl   Idiot. I've got AIDS. If I even scratch you, you'll die. So . . .

Vlad   Go fuck yourself. Got it, bitch?

Girl   You haven't understood, idiot. I almost died now. I've come back from the dead. If . . .

Vlad   Go fuck yourself. Isn't that clear? She's come back from the dead. How is it there, by the way? Judging by you, you don't get paid there either?

Girl   No. You don't.

Vlad   And that's because money's from the devil. Do you get it? Everything that kills us is from God.

Girl   And murderers?

Vlad   Even murderers.

Girl   And drugs?

Vlad   Even drugs, and music, and books. And dreams. Everything, everything that brings us closer to our mortality. Because after death we go to Him. And everything that distances us from death is from the devil. Everything.

Girl   Money's from the devil?

Vlad   Money. The management. The president. Television. You say you almost died?

Girl   I came back to life.

Vlad   And now you need money? Did you come back to life for that?

Girl   Fuck knows.

Vlad   I know you. I was in the same car as you. You smelt of snow. You looked different, you were shining. The way that Christmas toys shine. So?

Girl So what?

Vlad Nothing. Go on, fuck off.

Vlad shuts the door to the cabin. The girl stands for some time by the door, then leaves.

VII. THE DREAM

Vlad's flat. He's lying on the floor, on his back, making out the sky through the ceiling. Vlad lives in a high-rise building, and above his ceiling are some twenty other ceilings – but Vlad doesn't give a damn. He can make out the sky, so that's fucking fine. Alla sits on the sofa. She turns off the television. The sky above Vlad becomes much clearer, and he smiles.

Alla So, little one? Did you have a good walk?

Vlad I did...

Alla Did you understand what people need?

Vlad I did...

Alla And what was it? I'm interested myself...

Vlad Money. Almost everyone needs money. In other words, they think they need money.

Alla And you?

Vlad Me? I don't need anything any more. I've got everything.

Alla Really?

Vlad Uh-huh.

Alla Everything-everything?

Vlad Everything. I have everything, both from the devil and from God. I have absolutely everything that I need. It's just that – unlike other people – I realise that.

Alla And others don't realise that?

Vlad Of course, they don't. Otherwise they would have . . . done something a long time ago.

Alla Done what?

Vlad Never mind. Alla, have any of your dreams remained? Ones from your childhood?

Alla I don't really know . . . you'll laugh, but I always dreamt most about money. You know the game when all the kids get together and imagine what they'd do if they had a magic wand.

Vlad And you said that you'd make money? Lots and lots?

Alla Uh-huh. And then I'd buy things for everyone. Clothes, flats, parents for those who didn't have them, loads for myself . . .

Vlad "Zillions of things".

Alla Huh?

Vlad "Zillions of things". That's what we always said as children.

Alla Maybe. I can't remember anymore.

Vlad Do you know what I dreamt about most?

Alla What?

Vlad That . . . never mind.

Alla What?

Vlad How about doing something else?

Alla (*coquettishly*) What?

Vlad (*coquettishly*) Exactly.

Alla screws up her eyes and looks at Vlad – and her eyes shine through her almost-closed eyelashes. Vlad leans lower, pressing his cheek to the rough surface of her tights. Vlad rubs his cheek against her, the tights whisper and Alla moves her legs slightly apart – her eyelashes tremble but Vlad doesn't see that (unfortunately). Vlad touches Alla's inner thighs with the ends of his fingers – her legs move apart and he sees the glittering of her knickers because it's dark there. Vlad breathes in, Alla hears his breathing and responds with hers, turns on the music system which is her last conscious action.

Because her childhood dream is also what Vlad is now doing. He kisses Alla's legs, just above her tights, her stomach is moving right next to his face. Alla breathes, Vlad breathes, as if there is nothing besides this breathing, though in fact there is – hands take hold of other hands, fingers intertwine with other fingers, music centre green light slow beautiful movements. Then Vlad runs the end of his tongue along Alla's back, making her feel each vertebra like a knob of butter, like the seed of a fruit in a sponge cake. Alla lifts up her thighs. She looks past Vlad's shoulders – there's nothing there, just the wall, but something is swimming on the wall, something is blossoming right there on the wallpaper, real flowers, plastic – and because of that – bright fish from the shop.

She sighs happily and immediately relaxes her neck. Vlad kisses her breasts, they are small, immediately hard and small and moving rhythmically. Vlad catches the twists in Alla's body, drinks in the space of a living body like a bitter sea wave. A miracle is happening in each second of this time – they accept this, they live in these feelings as if in a place.

Vlad rubs his hands down her sides. She strokes his hands with her own. Snow and coffee beans. Summer on the new carpet (a realisation that how much it costs matters less than what's happening on it). Vlad rubs Alla. He dies and beats feverishly, Alla feels his death, she puts her hand between his legs and helps him, pressing his penis and pushing it into herself, right into her gap, between her legs. Vlad grabs Alla by the hair and violently pulls her head backwards and to the side. He bites her neck. He crushes her breasts in his fist. She pushes her nails into his back. He arches his back, pressing his thighs into her, turning them, spinning, twisting in, almost pushing right through her and pulsating in her very clitoris.

Alla opens her mouth. He kisses her. She is short of breath. She shakes her head and her hair is everywhere, Vlad shakes his head and begins to beat his penis in her cunt. Beating and beating, until Alla begins to sigh happily and whisper something – in a rhythm, turning into words which could have been said, or more likely not. Because Vlad suddenly takes his penis out of Alla and drops down between her legs and sucks her clitoris and licks her as if he was possessed (he really wants to drink), Alla strokes the back of his head and tries to see with wide open eyes how the beautiful flowers were swimming there, but Vlad touches a small salty button with the end of his tongue and Alla groans, and the noise interrupts the flowers, and the room grows darker and it suddenly becomes like when – a little girl – she touched herself secretly, and unexpectedly flowed over, her legs grew weak, her hands shook just a little, and she didn't tell anyone, and he is moving around her little crack, all around anywhere his tongue can find, and by now nothing matters, whatever you want however you want, whatever you want however you want, and Vlad again puts his penis and fucks with hard, flexible movements as if he became twice the length, but not wider, just longer, because it's exactly the same just lo-o-onger, and Alla comes, feverishly pressing his penis with two fingers, and then Vlad puts his finger in her mouth and she licks it and he licks it, and Vlad presses the little area between the genitals and the bum twice (he was holding his penis at the very upper area and pressing the clitoris, when he pushed hard, when everything streamed out from within) and he comes and everything pours out into Alla, Vlad feels lumps and liquids moving further there, as if they are dissolving there inside, and before everything pours out, he takes out his penis and touches it to Alla, to her stomach, then he brings it down and the final push is straight into her clitoris, and Alla comes again.

They fall asleep. Time passes. They wake up.

Alla Where are you going?

Vlad Do you want something to drink?

Alla Desperately. Can I have it with ice? I don't care what, as long as it's with ice . . . okay?

Vlad Of course. (*He stops by the door.*) Allochka?

Alla Mm?

Vlad No doors. No windows. No country. No earth. Nothing. Just – the World. The whole world. For us. For everyone. For you. For everyone-everyone . . . Hm?

Alla What's that?

Vlad I made it up. A long, long time ago. When I was small. That's how it was. For a while. And do you know what happened afterwards?

Alla What?

Vlad Afterwards, everything suddenly became tiny, tiny . . . really tiny. And everything became not for everyone anymore. Everything was only for some people. *That's* for someone. *That's* for someone else. And *that's* not for anyone any more.

Alla Was that a dream?

Vlad To make the world big. Big again. It's simple.

Alla Yes? How?

Vlad There's a way. Lie down, I'll bring you something to drink.

Vlad, smiling, goes into the kitchen. Everything is ready there – buckwheat, dry sausage, condensed milk, coffee. He gets dressed, collects his rucksack, mixes a cocktail for Alla. He puts some ice in it. He comes back in and puts it beside her.

Alla Ah . . . oh, God, where are you going? Vlad, not again . . . Vlad, why . . .

Vlad Sssssh . . . quiet. It's not for ever. It's only for a while. I have to, do you understand, I have to – all dreams come true. They have to come true. It's essential that they do, because then they are added to the world . . . something is added. And the world becomes bigger. Even if we have less. Yes?

He goes. While Vlad prepares for his war, the girl waits for Yuri outside a court. They sit on a bench. Yuri drinks a beer. The girl smokes.

Girl How much?

Bloke Three years, on probation. Like the man said. It's fine.

Girl I didn't wait for the sentence.

Bloke Whatever. I don't care.

Girl What are we going to do?

Bloke Shall we go to yours?

Girl What's at mine?

Bloke You've got a bed.

Girl So?

Bloke Well, it's cool. A bed's more comfortable, much better than a hallway . . .

Girl Idiot! . . .

They kiss. The bloke throws the unfinished bottle into the bin so he can hold the girl with both hands.

Girl Have you changed your mind about Siberia?

Bloke I've changed my mind. Siberia – my arse. It's also Siberia here. We'll get a place, as long as it has a gas stove . . .

Girl Why do we need a gas stove?

Bloke We'll turn off all the electricity.

Girl But how will we listen to music?

Bloke With batteries.

Girl Ah . . . where will we get so many batteries?

Bloke We'll make homebrew. It's the right time of year for it. We'll make loads of money – fuck, it's a dying art, almost nobody else is doing it. We'll be there only ones in the market – there's be loads of fucking money.

Girl I . . . have to tell you a something.

Bloke What?

Girl I met this one guy, not long ago . . . well, I wanted to rob him, the way you taught me, well, when you take a syringe and tell them you've got AIDS . . .

Bloke So? What happened?

Girl He told me a wicked thing about money.

Bloke What was it?

Girl Money's from the devil.

Bloke Yeah, everyone knows that anyway.

Girl And music is from God.

Bloke Well? So what?

Girl Let's earn enough only to listen with batteries and eat something. Yes?

Bloke Of course.

Girl Yes?

Bloke Of course.

Girl Nice.

Bloke Now tell me about you.

Girl What about me? . . . ah, I almost died . . . seriously . . . a real return of the living corpses . . .

The street. The summer. The watchman carefully takes bits of rubbish off the grass.

VIII. THE VICTORY

Vlad is listening to a voice recording which he has made earlier:

By writing books.

By drawing.

By thinking up medicines.

By reaching new physical heights.

By observing the sun bending over to the old fence.

By kissing with sunflower seeds.

By boiling fish-soup.

By breakfasting.

By singing.

By beating our fists against the walls.

Through our teeth.

Towards the horizon.

By loving and dreaming.

Just by speaking simple words.

He switches the Dictaphone off, and then puts it into recording mode.

Vlad (*speaking into the Dictaphone*) There are many of us. There are many of us, listen to me. we are all different. We live properly. We live properly. There are many of us, even we don't know how many of us there are. And we know what we need. We need a river, stars. The cosmos at night. When you tilt your head back . . . looking high up . . . it's so high up. And we know that happiness is up there. But the management comes from the devil. Because they spit on the cosmos.

He is clutching a small radio loudspeaker in his hand.

Vlad But inside they are dead. That's why they teach us to die aswell. Because if we aren't dying – we won't working for them. We won't earn money for them. But, actually, nobody is dying. NOT ONE PERSON IS DYING. We are made differently. Each of us. Each person who wishes. Each person who intends. Each person who looks at the sunset, who smokes on a balcony, who cleans their teeth, who tidies up their papers and that's each of us, each of us, each of us. They are taking everything away from us. From everybody. But they can also be killed.

Vlad puts down all of his worldly possessions. He picks up a gun and leaves the dilapidated house, this commune.

At the same time, Vlad is walking along a corridor.

IX. STEPS ALONG A CORRIDOR

Vlad walks along a corridor. He is smoking. The corridor is long and dim. It is impossible to tell where the walls end and the floor begins – everything is made from one and the same material. There are no doors leading out of the corridor. At the end of the corridor, unbearably far, blinks an old luminescent lamp. Someone touches Vlad's sleeve. He looks down. It's a boy, he stops and looks at him attentively.

Boy Where are you going?

Vlad shows him.

Vlad Over there.

Boy I know that place. There are big beautiful houses there. Expensive ones.

Vlad Where are you going?

Boy There.

Vlad It's not bad there, either.

Boy There's a small playground with a roundabout. It's not much fun. I tried everything out the first time I was there so now I know it's not much fun.

Vlad Why are you going then?

Boy Because they're waiting for me.

X. YOU MUST NOT DIE

THE END

DREAMS

by

Natalia Koliada

A story of love and betrayal

Based on real events

Dedicated to Ira

THE CHARACTERS

Maria – 45 years old

Anna – 30 years old

Elena – 58 years old

Olga – 43 years old

Tatiana – 30 years old

Melissa – 49 years old

Inside a nice flat: a christmas trees stands in the living room, the hallway is decorated for a celebration. There is quiet music playing. The door-bell rings. Maria comes out into the hallway, goes over to the door and opens it.

Anna

Olga } *Me-rry Christ-mas!*

Tatiana

They embrace and congratulate the hostess.

Anna Why so glum?

Maria Well, I . . . Hey, where's Lena? . . .

Olga Her grandsons arrived . . . Why's the music so funereal? Is today a celebration or not?

Maria It's Bach . . .

Olga Whatever . . . We need something more cheerful . . .

Tatiana (*to Maria*) Don't pay any attention to her. They've decided we're going to party today and no-one's to argue . . . you know them . . .

The women who have arrived take off their winter layers and shoes during the conversation and put on slippers. They are all dressed beautifully and elegantly.

Maria You look beautiful!

Anna Exactly. Go and get dressed.

Maria It's not right –

Olga Cut it out! You've got fifteen minutes . . .

Maria Alright, alright . . .

Tatiana That didn't take long!

Maria goes into her room.

Olga (*after her*) And change the music!

Tatiana Don't start . . . change it yourself.

Olga Let's put on something life-affirming.

Olga and Anna sit down in the armchairs. Tatiana changes the music. A beautiful Christmas melody begins to play.

Tatiana There . . . that's festive . . .

Anna Even though we're alone –

Olga Better not to start –

Anna True . . . Or we'll end the celebrations before we even began . . . Although, what sort of a Christmas is it when –

Tatiana I knew it!

Anna You wouldn't understand –

Tatiana But I've –

Maria walks back into the room.

Maria I hope I didn't get dressed for nothing.

Tatiana *That* is mm-hm! And just in time . . .

Maria I've only got wine and snacks, *zakuski* . . .

Olga That'll do.

Maria goes off into the kitchen.

Maria (*off*) Open the champagne! . . . I'll bring the rest!

Anna opens the champagne and pours it into the glasses which are set out on the counter. Maria comes into the living room with a tray, full of zakuski *(snacks).*

Olga Here, we can help . . .

Tatiana Yeah . . .

They put the dishes with zakuski on the counter.

Tatiana (*to Maria*) We're at your command!

Maria There's nothing else to do . . . we can drink champagne and –

Olga I'll make a toast! Let's drink to justice! If you wish for something at Christmas – it comes true . . . Miracles do happen, you know . . .

Maria Okay! To justice!

Anna It's not the first Christmas we've wished for that –

Tatiana Down in one!

They clink glasses and drink.

Maria Ladies, please make yourselves at home . . . the evening is long, the champagne is flowing –

Olga That's for sure.

Anna If someone had told me three years ago that I'd be having Christmas here . . .

Maria I've been thinking that for years . . . Why us? . . .

Tatiana I had an operation when I was nineteen and I was told that I wouldn't have children . . . It was awful! I thought that the world had shrunk and why should I be suffering . . . for everyone . . . They're absolutely different things of course but . . .

Olga A *g-r-eat* start to the evening.

Maria I read somewhere that grief pours down from the sky into one place and that people walk into it, completely randomly, into that circle . . .

Tatiana And happiness?

Maria Happiness comes for a reason.

Anna Well, I mean, we've been in the circle . . . So when are we getting happiness?

Olga When it's the right time! Like Tanyushka got that news – she gave birth to a daughter . . .

Maria And what a daughter . . . And it'll definitely come to you, Olga.

Anna But probably not for me and Maria.

Tatiana Okay! Last chance to have a fun evening . . . Everyone will tell a story about their first love. And if anyone doesn't have a good one, then you'll have to make it up!

Anna We know all about that.

Maria Then let's have another.

Maria pours the champagne.

Maria Let's drink to being together . . . and to friends who support us and understand us!

They all clink glasses and drink.

Tatiana Anya, you start . . .

Anna Very funny! Why me?

Tatiana Because it will be your turn at some point anyway.

Anna Iron logic.

Maria So start.

Anna (*after a pause*) Well, look . . . Love first struck me at primary school . . . Or rather, even before primary school. There was a boy living in the same building as us and I liked him a lot. I was pining after him secretly and thought that I loved him even though we had never spoken – I had only seen him in the courtyard . . .

Olga Love at first sight?

Anna Well, something like that . . .

Maria And then what, you never met him?

Tatiana Just listen, you're not meant to ask questions –

Anna Exactly . . . Then it was time for primary school. My brother went to the school to find out what class I was in. He came back and told me it was class "I" . . . So I went, on the first of September to class "I" and I wasn't on the list . . .

Olga And?

Anna The teachers began to work it out and realised I was meant to be in class "J". It's just my brother mixed up the letters "I" and "J" . . . And so I went into the class I was meant to be in . . . I went in and . . .

Maria Well? Don't drag it out!

Anna And I see that boy! But I also saw my best friend . . . And I felt relieved: my friend and my love would be beside me for many long years. That was happiness!

Tatiana It happens . . . and you were so sceptical . . .

Olga Your friend didn't steal the boy . . . ?

Maria Now, now, Olga . . . And how did it all end?

Anna With a wedding, obviously.

They laugh.

Olga (*turning to Maria*) Oh, come on . . . Were you forgetting what age she was?

Maria So what? As you know, love conquers all ages.

Tatiana Who's next? Go on, Olga, you go.

Olga How about Maria?

Anna Do it without thinking – like me.

Maria Okay, okay. I'll help you out and you can think of something, in the meantime.

Tatiana You know what, let's make the question harder each time someone answers one.

Anna That's not fair! I had to talk about love and they'll get to talk about any old rubbish.

Olga Perfect, let's drink to that.

Maria (*smiling*) You didn't have anything to say anyway.

Anna Cut it out, you.

Tatiana Okay! New task: the most vivid memory from your childhood.

Maria Oh, there's enough of them!

Anna I told you mine was the hardest.

Tatiana takes the champagne bottle and fills their glasses.

Tatiana To first love?

Maria Excellent toast! You've all heard about my first love already . . . Anya, don't get upset, I'll tell you about my adulthood love later . . .

Anna Thank you, we know about that already. It's a headline story.

Maria My most vivid childhood memory? . . . It's like a ray of sunshine in my mind. . . . (*Pause*) Probably, the trips to the circus.

Olga *To the circus?*

Maria You wouldn't understand. Only people who have grown up in the countryside can understand . . . (*Pause*) A trip to the circus took a whole day: we were lent a small bus from mum's work, we all squeezed inside it and went to the capital with our parents.

Anna And do you remember what you saw?

Maria Uh-uh.

Anna So what's so vivid about it? The bus?

Maria . . . At the circus, we bought ice cream and the sweets "Misha the slopey-pawed bear" and we were all dressed up . . . Such funny, smartly dressed, little . . . (*Pause*) That was happiness!

Olga Is that it?

Maria No, the most interesting things happened on the way back – we would stop in the woods. My parents would get out some bread, cucumbers, sweets which they had bought in the city . . . Our parents would have something to drink and we would eat "Doctor's Own" boiled sausage . . . Everyone felt so good! . . . (*Pause*) We were happy! I used to think that such happiness could only exist in our country.

Tatiana What else?

Maria Also – the neighbours . . . a Jewish family . . . They had an important part in bringing me up and they were always very caring towards me . . . Their granny cooked wonderful Jewish dishes . . . more than anything I loved when she prepared *bonda* – the Jewish bread made of potatoes . . . something half way between our potato pie and rye bread. It was a distinctive colour, a type of . . . grey . . . I'll never forget that taste.

Tatiana Wonderful.

Olga Nobody knows as a child what they'll remember for the rest of their life . . .

Anna (*sighing*) What about our children?

Pause.

Tatiana And now . . .

Olga Yes, it's our dear toast-master's turn!

Tatiana No, I should go last.

Olga Where's that written down?

Anna Olya, it's really too much.

Tatiana That's fine . . . what shall I tell you?

Olga Tell us what sort of an upbringing you had?

Tatiana A-ah . . . (*Pause*) My dad.

Olga Meaning?

Tatiana Literally. If I did something wrong, mama would say the phrase which would turn my legs to jelly and make my insides go cold.

Maria What was it?

Tatiana "Tatiana, go to your father's study".

Everyone laughs.

Tatiana It's funny now. But then I'd beg my mum to convince my dad not to call me in to see him. I would tearfully promise never to repeat my bad behaviour . . .

Olga And what happened in the study?

Tatiana I don't know, I never had to go.

Everyone laughs.

Olga Well, that's quite a method. Do you know what I want to tell you –

Anna Oh, suddenly you have something to say?

Olga They're all the same.

Tatiana Parents?

Olga Men!

Anna Where did that come from!

Maria Why are you saying that?

Olga Yes, only men can treat children that way. Just think about yours . . .

Pause.

Tatiana Do you think this is the right conversation?

Maria (*to Olga*) Don't worry. Since you've already started, you may as well . . .

Anna I remember being pleasantly surprised by Dima. It happened when I gave birth to my little boy. Dima wanted to take all the night duties on himself and decided that I shouldn't get up for the child but that he'd do it himself . . . The night went by and he got up to take care of Yurik who was crying . . . He tried to feed him and change his nappy, carried him in his arms but Yurik kept crying. I wasn't sleeping, of course, but I gave him the chance to do something nice for me, which is all he wanted to do . . . He suffered through the night and when it was almost morning, he came to me, all wet, and said: "That's enough! Take him!" . . . He didn't manage but it was good to see him try.

Olga That's what I said. They can't do anything.

Tatiana I completely disagree.

Maria Me, too. My little ones have more in common with their father.

Anna You mean "had more in common"?

Maria Well! If we're going to start . . .

Tatiana (*interrupting*) Go on, tell us. I'm curious . . . We have the same thing in my family.

Olga Well, we've already heard how you were brought up.

Tatiana Tell us, Maria.

Maria I always had the feeling that he knew their problems better than me . . . He knew everything: where they were, who they were with, when they were out . . . Somehow he could easily work out what was important to the children in any situation. (*Pause. Smiling.*) They had a very difficult adolescence . . . (*Pause*) He knew all their boyfriends –

Tatiana That's impressive –

Maria . . . And even helped these boyfriends with their career choices. And I never had enough of an attention span or enough energy for that . . . Although now I would.

Pause.

Once he goes to the younger one's school . . . to a parent's evening . . . It was the first time he went to a school in ten years . . . And the teacher starts saying all sorts of rubbish: your girl is hyperactive – she makes rude comments to her classmates, she should try to work harder, so I've given her term grade as two out of five . . . He listened for about five minutes and then says: "You know, I've come here for the first time and it's possible I won't have time to come to another parents' evening. So I'd like you to tell me something good about my daughter". The teacher was stunned, didn't know what to say . . . And then forced herself to say something positive . . . Well, we've chatted enough . . . Time to light the Christmas tree . . . and to open another champagne . . .

Tatiana Although my girls are still young but my husband is also –

Anna Well done, you – putting up a Christmas tree! There was me . . .

Maria You know, it was just habit . . . It's not a big effort . . . Christmas trees . . . you just unpack it from a box and there it is.

Olga Still, well done . . . Well done for getting us together today . . . Do you remember a couple of years ago when we were at some reception and then you suggested going back to yours?

Maria Of course, I remember . . . There wasn't a damn thing at home . . . vodka, bread and gherkins.

Olga But it was great fun . . .

Anna We're a bit like disabled people . . . They can also discuss their issues between themselves without worrying that they're being misunderstood . . .

Maria Although it was a painful time . . .

Anna It's a shame Elena's not with us –

Tatiana Grandchildren. Family is sacred –

Anna I'm grateful to her. She always told me what to do –

Maria The main thing is you're here . . . also let's not forget Melissa . . . (*Smiling*). You could say we're the perfect women's collective . . .

Anna . . . For an international tour.

Olga There's something I don't quite get. Is today Christmas or some other occasion?

Maria True . . . Why are we all so . . . come on . . . for us . . . for our love . . . for the worthy and dedicated men . . .

Olga Let's drink to them!

Anna Yes, Olga . . . you're lucky . . .

Maria For love!

They clink glasses.

Tatiana And what a beginning –

Maria That's when we met –

Olga I was about to meet Andrei . . .

Anna And we were about to travel, that was about two weeks to go . . .

A bright flash of light. Six chairs on stage. It seems to be an office. Melissa and Tatiana sit on the chairs.

Melissa Two weeks isn't enough . . . . I don't think I can help you . . .

Tatiana You can.

Melissa I don't know . . .

Tatiana Melissa, you *have* to help them . . .

Melissa Yes, I know that. But these aren't normal students. Normally it's simple but I keep remembering who they are and –

Tatiana Why think about that? Treat them like you would anyone else. And that will be easier for them, too . . . You can just explain that it will help them . . . with the restoration of justice . . .

Melissa I don't know . . . Can you actually imagine how difficult it will be for them . . .

Tatiana After all they've lived through –

Melissa That's what I'm talking about – they will have to live through it again, time after time –

Tatiana Luckily, only with words –

Melissa It's the same thing.

A knock at the door.

Maria (*opening the door*) Well, hello! . . . Here we are! . . . May we?

Melissa Yes, yes – of course . . . Come in . . . We got carried away, chatting . . .

Maria, Elena, Olga come in to the room. They sit down on the chairs.

Tatiana Sit down. Is Anna on her way?

Maria I think so . . . I called her yesterday . . . She promised to come . . . although it's hard for her . . . less time has gone by for her . . . But she's a smart girl and she understands this is necessary . . .

Tatiana A year – that's a big difference . . .

The door opens, Anna comes in.

Anna Were you talking about me?

Tatiana Yes . . . Maria was trying to convince me that you'd come.

Anna Sorry I'm late.

Melissa Well, then . . . shall we begin? Now – each person shall briefly tell a story on any subject . . .

Maria Can we talk about our childhoods?

Melissa Early childhood?

Maria Not exactly . . .

Melissa Please pay attention to the cards . . . . Remember: green – the first part is finished, yellow – the main part . . . red – the final part.

Maria Yes, I remember. Well, I'll begin?

Melissa Yes, please.

Maria When I was in the first year at school, I had a neighbour – he was called Sasha. I always had a good time with him. Sometimes, when we played at home, in a outburst of emotion he always hugged me around my neck and shouted: "I love you!" But I pushed him away and shouted; "You idiot! You idiot!"

Melissa shows the green card. Maria nods slightly in response to show that she has seen it.

Maria When we were walking to school, he would say to me: "Promise me that you won't misbehave today!" I would reply grandly: "I promise!" We would come to the classroom and the lesson would begin. I couldn't bear the moralising tone of our teacher for long and I would begin to add my own little comments.

After she'd had enough of my sarcastic comments, she'd say threateningly: "You'll stay behind after class today!" I had to stay behind to write something or read something. And Sasha always stayed in the corridor – he waited until they let me go home . . . When the teacher's colleague came in, she'd ask: "What's going on here?" The teacher would always reply: "She's staying behind after class and that boy is waiting for her." . . . After class, Sasha and I would go home where his mum would feed us and we'd do our homework together . . . Then they left . . . Mum told me to go and say goodbye. I went and said the phrase I'd been taught: "Have a safe journey!" And he threw himself at me, hugged me around the neck and began shouting: "Maria, I love you!". And I gave my traditional reply: "You idiot!"

Melissa shows the yellow card.

Maria Unfortunately, I never saw him again. He was probably my first love, I just didn't know what that was, at the time . . .

Melissa (*smiling, shows the red card*) Thank you. We'll stop there for now. Funny. And more importantly it had substance . . . You're ready to speak publicly . . .

Maria Yes? Thanks.

Melissa Well, let's go on. Maybe someone wants to tell a story from their adult life?

Anna Can I?

Melissa About what?

Anna About my family . . .

Melissa About your parents?

Anna No, about my son and my husband . . . Is that okay?

Melissa Of course . . .

Anna (*sighing heavily*) Every girl dreams about a prince riding up to her on a white horse and bathing her in flowers . . . in tenderness . . . in kisses . . . My husband was one of those men who only say "I love you" once in their life . . . and then never again. Now I understand that men like that . . . are the most trust-worthy . . .

Melissa shows the green card.

Anna The model of our family life was not based, as the psychologists say, on the same model of family life as that of our parents. We tried to do things our own way. Our relationships were so intelligent that we couldn't even allow ourselves to use rude words . . . Even when we were making jokes. Everyone was surprised – because we got married so young – how we managed to stay together . . . . It's just we learnt to give each other room . . .

Melissa shows the yellow card.

Anna To love is one thing but to give way and be tolerant is another side of family relations. If it works, then people who love one another, in the language of fairy-tales, "will live happily ever after and die quietly one day" . . . (*Sighing*). So that's the way it is . . .

Melissa (*shows the red card*). Yes-ssss, you're already talking better than professional speakers . . . It seems you're ready to go on to the main subjects . . .

Pause.

Melissa Who will try? Olga, or you, Elena?

Elena I'm not ready yet. I can make a joke of something serious . . . But I don't see any sense in that . . .

Melissa Then, Olga, seems that it's your turn.

Olga (*prepares for a moment*) I'm called Olga. I'm 43 years old. I have two wonderful children. One is 16 years old. The eldest is called Irina, the youngest is Svetik. This is my second marriage. My husband is an incredible, energetic man. He's just a volcano . . . Wherever he is, he changes everything . . .

Melissa shows the green card.

Olga Well, what else. We were running a business together.

Melissa (*shaking her head*). Only about yourself.

Olga Yes, I know. It's just hard . . . the people closest to me –

Melissa I understand. But, to start with –

Elena (*interrupts Melissa with irritation*). Forgive me for saying so but if you think this is easy then you're mistaken.

Melissa I don't think that . . . I only want to help you . . . I understand that you sometimes feel offended by us . . . (*Short pause*). The framework of our meetings is pretty strict but there's no other way. Unfortunately, we don't have five years to learn public speaking . . .

Maria There are two weeks left.

Tatiana We will be with you at all the meetings – you won't be alone . . . No need to worry about that . . .

Melissa Let's at least try . . . I understand that nobody can force you to do what you don't want to but you should understand that it's important for them . . .

Pause.

Olga It's just hard to begin.

Maria So that's exactly what you have to do.

Melissa As soon as you shift the "rock", you'll start to feel so much better . . . and everything will change . . .

A flash of light. Maria's flat. Christmas continues.

Maria Everything changed since then . . . although, it didn't happen very long ago . . .

Olga It doesn't matter how long ago it was . . .

Anna We were so awkward then . . .

Maria Yes! . . . Whenever I saw a journalist, I became feverish.

Anna That's true . . . I felt like my blood had gone cold in my veins . . .

Maria Every time they told me there would be a press conference or an interview, I grabbed a sheet of paper and began to write out my speech. Then from that I summarised the main arguments . . . And then from the summary, I wrote out only the most important points . . . And I jotted them down in a notebook so I wouldn't miss anything . . . My God, like a school girl . . .

Tatiana Yes, I was always surprised by your diligence . . . Well, you're still the same now, actually . . . (*Short pause*). How did you cope with all the endless meetings with journalists? I can't imagine –

Maria I'm grateful to them, you know.

Tatiana For what?

Maria I had to say what had happened so many times that I began to fully understand the situation for myself. I had new ideas and a different perspective of the problem . . . I began to see my role in a different way . . . Talking to them changed me . . . (*A short pause*). Although some journalists are bastards –

Olga Only journalists? What about the people who rant against us for making these trips –

Anna I wouldn't wish it on them, to have to make trips abroad . . . They'll never understand what it is to tell your own story an infinite number of times . . . and to live it over and over again . . .

Pause.

Maria It seems we forgot that today is Christmas . . .

Tatiana (*lifts her glass of champagne*) Here's to all of you!

Anna We are always ready to drink to that toast –

Olga With the greatest of pleasure!

They all clink glasses and drink.

Maria Well done us! We've did things well, even at the beginning . . .

Olga We even managed to afford some small celebrations . . .

Anna Well, yes . . . by ourselves . . .

Maria Yes, by ourselves . . . So what?! Should we have invited some guests to tell them our story?! Even my friends sob when I start to remember something . . . It's not right . . . Why should anyone have to live our lives? . . . (*A short pause*). It's my life . . . mine.

Tatiana Elena said something once: "We can't have private lives"
. . .

Anna Perhaps she's right . . .

Maria My God . . . I'd give everything to have my old life back, not this . . . "public duty". However much I didn't want to get involved, I had to . . .

A sharp black out. A bright light. The room where the women are sitting.

Melissa And we have to start some time. The sooner we begin, the quicker we'll succeed . . .

Olga The last time I didn't manage to finish . . . So let me start this time.

Melissa Okay.

Olga From the beginning?

Melissa Yes.

Olga It's hard . . . Although perhaps it's easier for me anyway than for the others . . . (*Short pause.*) I already told you about my children . . .

Melissa No, no! From the very beginning, please, and strictly by the cards.

Olga (*after a deep sigh*) My country is in the centre of Europe. The most wonderful people live there. And I . . . live there, too. I have two wonderful children and a lovely husband. He's a businessman. He builds houses in which people live . . . (*sighing lightly*) many happy people . . . The same types of family as mine . . .

Melissa shows a green card.

Olga (*continues to talk more emotionally not paying attention to Melissa*) We celebrated birthdays and public holidays properly . . . and we worked together . . . Also he's . . . a deputy . . . of the last real parliament. (*Olga begins to raise her voice*). But he was one of the initiators of the impeachment . . .

Melissa shows the yellow card.

Olga (*getting lost in her memories*) How did it all happen? . . . It was morning . . . As usual, we got up, ate breakfast and left . . . Well, yes, it was morning . . . (*She begins to cry quietly*) . . . They're just shitheads . . . They arrested us right outside the house! Just like that . . . outside the house . . . (*A short pause*). I told him, don't get involved in it . . . There are 75 people who signed it . . . There wasn't a first or last . . . They drew a circle around the paper and signed around the circle . . . But they arrested my husband . . . . They let me go – but not him. (*A short pause*). We have children at home . . . I'm alone . . . There's an unbearable feeling of loneliness . . . He got four years . . . Immediately we had almost no friends . . . . (*She begins to come back to herself*). Thank God, there's all of you . . . What am I saying? . . . I'm so sorry . . . It just came out in a mess . . .

Maria Don't worry, relax . . . There's only two weeks left . . . When he comes back it will all be different . . .

A flash of light. Christmas.

Maria It wasn't like that at all! When he was released, he took us to a restaurant. Do you really not remember that?

Olga Of course. You're right.

Maria I was asking you even then "Olga, do you believe this?" . . . Do you remember?

Anna And you replied: "No."

Tatiana It was unbelievable.

Olga After so many years of horror . . . .

Anna As he put it –

Maria (*in a deep voice*) Girls! I owe you! Today we've got a celebration on our hands!

Olga We drank ridiculously expensive wine . . .

Anna And ate delicious food . . .

Maria What happiness! Like the feelings of emptiness had just lifted . . . for one evening.

Anna And I thought it was only me . . .

A bright flash of light. All six women are in the office. Elena stands separate to the others.

Elena I have a husband . . . I'm called Elena. I'm the wife of . . .

Elena starts to cry but continues to talk. She wipes the tears with her hand. Melissa quietly gives her a tissue. Elena wipes away the tears with the tissue. The light goes out sharply. A flash of light. The beam of light catches Elena who wipes a tear away with a tissue – next to her is the silhouette of a man dressed in a doctor's uniform.

Doctor Forgive me . . . I haven't come out of intensive care for forty-eight hours . . . My assistant told me that you're still here . . . You're . . .

Elena (*crying quietly*) Yes, I'm . . . I'm . . . his wife . . . Elena . . . He was everything to me . . . Our son is a spitting image of him . . . as tall . . . as big . . . He's kind. (*Elena falls silent for a moment*). I'm sorry . . . My husband . . . He's strong, don't worry about that . . . He can cope with much worse things . . . He's a football referee and . . . a member of the Academy of Sciences . . . He was manager of a factory and the mayor . . . Everyone likes him . . . Why am I talking such rubbish?! (*Elena stands up suddenly and begins to talk loudly*). . . . I said that he could be killed! I said it but he said, "Don't worry, that's rubbish . . . " I said they would kill him (*she falls onto a chair, limply*) . . .

Doctor I'm sorry, I didn't want to . . . I thought you needed –

Elena (*shouts*) I don't need anything! I need my husband!! When can I see him?!

Doctor His condition is very serious . . .

The red light begins to flash with the word "intensive care".

Doctor Please excuse me . . .

Elena I'll go with you . . .

Doctor I'm sorry but you're not allowed in there.

Elena sits alone on the chair, with her head lowered and, clutching her hands together, she mutters.

Elena He just needs to rest a couple of days . . . And tomorrow he'll be with us again . . . he needs to rest . . . He got so tired the last few years . . . He needs to rest . . . He can stay here for a couple of days . . . Or even for a week . . .

The doctor comes in. Only his silhouette is lit up.

Doctor Elena . . .

Elena No . . . No, he hasn't died! (*Shouting*). No!!! (*Short pause*). He was killed!!! (*Shouting but more quietly than last time*). Do you understand? . . . My husband was killed!

A flash of light. Maria stands where Elena was standing.

Maria (*speaking very quietly*) My husband was killed . . . They killed the father of our two daughters . . . Last year was twenty-five years since our wedding . . . I had the anniversary without my husband . . . I see him now but only in my dreams . . . He was abducted . . . (*Pause*). That evening, I waited for my husband at home. He was with a friend . . . They loved to go to the sauna on Thursdays. They asked me to go with them that evening . . . But I was so tired . . . He usually came home at eleven after the sauna . . . But when it was already midnight . . .

Blackout. Flat. Maria sits in the darkness on a sofa. A table lamp is shining in the corner. Absolute darkness. An electronic alarm clock on the table begins to buzz with an unpleasantly piercing sound.

Maria (*jumps up from the sofa, runs over to the clock and begins to hit it*) Yes, I know, I know! . . . I know what time it is without you . . . (*Maria sits on the floor, picks up her mobile phone, dials a number, lifts the telephone to her ear and listens*) . . . . Why aren't you picking up? . . . (*Looks at her phone*). Well, why not?! (*She hears the noise of a passing car, Maria throws herself to the window and looks into the darkness*). Why is it so dark? . . . I can't see anything . . . (*She walks around the room, rolling her hands into her sweater*). Why is he so late? (*She dials a number again, listens, then again looks at the telephone*). I can't bear to hear this anymore. (*Pause. Maria turns to the audience.*) He always told me where he would be, always . . . Always! He taught me to do the same . . . (*Short pause*). You taught me to do the same!!! And now?! I'm scared . . . very scared . . . I understood that something had happened

. . . What?! What could have happened?! Why isn't your number responding? (*Picks up the phone and dials*). Hello, please tell me – you haven't seen him? . . . No? Please, help me . . . I've called all the police stations, the hospitals, the morgues . . . I can't find my husband . . .

Blackout. A bright flash of light. Maria stands in the same place where she began her story.

Melissa May I? I understand it's hard . . . But try to tell me about his abduction.

Maria They came out of the banya at around eleven . . . There was only an old woman who worked there at that time . . . She said: "Those lovely boys came out all clean . . . didn't drink . . . cracked a few jokes with me, said goodbye and left the banya, got in their car . . . " As soon as they drove around the corner, a car crossed their path . . . My husband reversed but another car blocked them from behind . . . The doors of our car always lock shut if you brake suddenly. The people who got out of the two cars surrounded the car and smashed in the side windows. (*Maria begins to cry*). They were dragged out . . . They were dragged out of the car across the broken glass . . . (*Pause*). The next day, they found blood where they were abducted . . . They were shoved into different cars and taken away. (*Maria calms down*). And out jeep stayed where it was – it was blocked. Later . . . they towed it away . . . Almost nothing else is known . . . But I know that they were shot . . . in the forest . . .

Blackout. A sharp flash of light. Maria is alone at home.

Maria Why isn't anybody calling? (*She lies down on the sofa, curls up in a ball and closes her eyes*). I feel cold inside . . . That can't have happened . . . because it can't have . . . They are in jail . . . They've been hidden in a psychiatric ward . . . (*Pause*). He will never come back . . . never come back . . .

A soft light. The door to the room opens – on the doorway stands the silhouette of a man.

Man I'm back . . .

Maria (*joyfully throws herself around his neck, hugs and kisses him*) God how long I've been looking for you! I've been waiting so long for you . . .

The light suddenly goes off.

Maria Where are you? . . . Where are you!! Where are you!!!

A flash of light. Maria stands in the middle of the room.

Maria I always told myself: "you should be a realist – in a dictatorship, people aren't abducted just to be detained". It was impossible to get used to that thought at first . . . I had to realise: what happened, happened. Sometimes, I allowed myself to reflect properly . . . and then I understood that he wasn't alive . . . But as soon as I realised that, my heart would stop beating . . . (*Pause*). I only found out about the worst things which had happened after the documents were published . . . The realisation happened gradually . . . and when it happened, I understood that it's better not to think about it at all . . . not at all . . . Because if you think about it – you could go mad. Was there anyone I didn't turn to for help . . . ?

A flash of light. Christmas.

Anna I think we all went to fortune-tellers and astrologers . . .

Maria And psychotherapists . . . I felt so low after the sessions and so drained . . . completely ill . . . So I gave up – I understood that I couldn't bear any more sessions.

Anna True . . . It seemed to get worse and worse . . . Or it didn't seem to – but actually became worse and worse . . .

Maria And people are kind . . . They honestly want to help you . . . I remember she said to me that I should start to live as if he had died. I couldn't even think about it . . . It's easy to say but just try it . . . (*Pause*). How do you convince yourself: "I'm going to live as if my husband has died".

Anna Only my family saved me . . .

Maria And I also began to read a whole load of books about traumatic psychological states . . . But theory is one thing – and the reality is . . . When you fall into a depression, you become another person. It's as if you understand – I need to stand up and walk but you can't move . . . A normal trip to the shop was just unbearable – to cross the square and go over to the shop, I had to summon up some sort of inhuman strength . . . It helped that I always had to do something. My responsibility to my family and to the upkeep of the house were mine: buy food, prepare meals, pay the bills . . . Probably that helped . . . Although it was so painful. (*Pause*). When I walked across that square – the feeling of loneliness just overwhelmed me . . . And that feeling of being split in two . . . I even talked to myself . . . There's a paradox: a psychologist dealing with traumatic states who can't get out of one herself . . .

Anna We could run seminars about trauma now, based on you as a case study. A vivid illustration . . .

Olga That's enough . . . A vivid illustration! . . .

Maria She's right . . . I remember when I first heard about . . . tens of thousands in Sri Lanka, in Kashmir . . .

Tatiana In Africa, Latin America . . .

Maria Do you remember the story . . . Well, there's the woman from Columbia whose husband –

Olga Yes, I do, I do –

Maria When she began to talk it was late in the evening, a woman asked her a question –

Anna If she knew where her husband was –

Maria I thought I'd faint –

Anna I started feeling ill as well . . . There are almost one hundred thousand missing people there . . .

Tatiana Why go that far for an example: just remember Chechnya . . .

Olga At least, everything has been sorted out in Ukraine . . . Even now it's hard to comprehend – how could this happen in the centre of Europe?

Tatiana There are evil people everywhere. You can't tell them apart from the colour of their skin or where they were born – they'll find you, wherever you are . . .

A flash of light. The office. All six women six on chairs. Anna gets up from her chair and goes into the centre.

Anna (*straightens her hair, looks around at the others*) It was evening . . . I was home . . . I called my husband's colleague . . . My husband should have met him at the airport . . . by car . . . (*Pause.*) My husband's colleague said that he was on his way . . . He'd never been to our home – and now he's telling me he's on his way . . . I felt that something had happened but I couldn't even think about that. I remember perfectly my thoughts at that moment: I thought that they want to fire my husband from his TV company . . . (*Pause*). They had suggested we move to Moscow to work there . . . I thought it wouldn't work out . . . I thought he had got nervous, got in his car and left . . . Why did I think that? (*Pause*). His friend told me . . . I can't put in words how I felt . . . The car was parked by the airport . . . Later . . . (*tears fall from her eyes, Anna wipes them away with tissues*). They found a spade with traces of his blood . . . I felt like it wasn't happening to me . . . That I'm having a nightmare . . . I couldn't sleep that night, I began to nod off towards the morning . . .

Light. Anna lies on her bed. Absolute silence. Suddenly we hear a man's voice.

Voice Anna, Anyuta, I'm cold . . .

Anna (*jumps up from bed and shouts*) They won't find him! They'll never find him!!! (*Falls to her knees*). Never! . . . They'll never find him! . . .

Light. The office. All the women rush to Anna.

Maria Anna! . . .

Melissa (*hugging Anna*). My poor girl . . .

Anna (*calming down*) Fine . . . . It's fine . . . I'll carry on . . .

Melissa Maybe it's not worth it.

Anna It has to happen one day . . . (*Pause*) I still can't understand why it happened . . . A day passed . . . He could have come back the following day, the day after . . . When I came to my senses, I asked my mum: "Why did I say it? That the door might suddenly open and he'll come in?" It was probably a whole year that I couldn't believe what had happened . . . For a year I was asking myself the same questions: "Why did they pick me, of all people? Why did this happen to me?" Like each of us . . . (*Pause*) My husband was a TV cameraman. He never picked up a gun and never harmed anyone but he was abducted and killed. It was done by a group of people who are called the "death squad". I don't know why they killed my husband, nor does my son, but a new part of my life began: nightmares, meaningless waiting, unbearable pain and despair. Probably, you have to live through something similar to understand something. But what? What should I understand?! That the most important thing in life is family?

A bright life. Christmas.

Maria Probably: family.

Anna My family did everything to keep me alive . . . If it wasn't for my family, I wouldn't have survived this. The thought that I didn't want to live was in my head everyday and it wouldn't leave –

Maria I stood in the metro a few times – the train was coming and I thought: "the best thing is to jump".

Tatiana And your children?

Olga *Well done*! And your children, your mother?

Maria Then I thought: what will happen to my mother? What will happen to my children? Where will they find money to live and pay for the flat? . . . And then I understood that I had to live so I could bring my children further from this horror.

Anna My family just took charge: someone would come every evening and sit with me.

Tatiana The nearest and dearest . . .

Maria Friends can be as close as family . . .

Olga That can happen but rarely.

Maria Tanya – my friend – was always beside me . . . Even if she wasn't there, then she'd call all the time. She dragged me along wherever she was going. It's very important because when you're at home alone and there's nobody with you – you could just go and kill yourself . . .

Tatiana It's typical . . . that most friends just vanish into thin air . . .

Maria We used to have people over . . . all the time, parties, drinks . . . and then suddenly no-one. And if someone was involved in business . . . it would suddenly turn out that there's no money . . . Everyone came to me, realising that I was the weak link . . . A blossoming company but suddenly "There's no money, you see . . . We were working off credit whereas your husband . . . ". I felt like a metal pole had been driven into me and I couldn't straighten up . . . it was completely cold inside. I couldn't sleep on my back, only on my side . . . I felt like someone was stopping me from straightening my body.

Tatiana Even now I don't understand how you recovered.

Anna When a year had passed, I understood that this is reality . . . that I need to live . . . I understood: if we don't do anything, the subject of the "disappeared" will just be forgotten . . . The time will pass and who, apart from me, will care about the fate of my husband? (*Short pause*). I was never interested in politics . . .

Maria . . . But we became interested in politics.

Anna What else could we do?

Pause.

Maria I owe it to them.

Olga What?

Maria I picked myself up with these words: "I owe it to my children, to my mum . . . ". I began to take care of my family: to buy food, to feed them . . . and to search for the truth . . .

Tatiana (*turning to Anna*) And how is your boy?

Anna He was nine years old then . . . He turned out to be very strong . . . He never tortured me with questions: "Where's dad? What happened?" He understood that something serious had happened but, seeing the state I was in, didn't ask any questions.

Maria I tried to hold myself in, in front of my children – not to cry, not to give in . . . I tried to keep our life the same as before, as much as possible, to make it easier for them.

Anna However many years go by, my boy still cries, even now, if he sees a film about people who disappear, who are unaccounted for.

Maria For me it's love scenes . . . I begin sobbing. My only joy was when I'd taken my youngest to his classes in the morning . . . I'd buy a newspaper, come back, drink coffee, read the newspaper – it was the only joy I had in life at that time. (*Pause*) My eldest was working . . . we didn't have any money . . . we had to live on almost nothing . . .

Anna Your friends helped you . . . but some people dropped me . . . altogether . . .

Tatiana Because they weren't real friends . . .

Anna Too true. Most of them weren't poor or struggling . . .

Maria Creditors turned up . . . they stripped the company . . .

Tatiana That doesn't have anything to do with friendship . . .

Maria Some of them were just scared . . . businessmen . . . On the one hand, they condemn the people who did this but on the other hand, . . . they're afraid . . . (*Pause*). Well, it doesn't matter . . . The main thing is my children supported me . . .

Anna My son always went with me to the demonstrations, he always said: "Mum, you don't have the right not to take me. I'll go anyway!"

Maria That's because he's from a new generation – they're not afraid of anything. Like my youngest: "You should do it. Who else will do it?" Not like my mum, when I was a child: "Don't say anything, don't go anywhere, you won't change anything . . . ".

Tatiana We panicked at home after every arrest. Mum thinks we will all be killed . . .

Anna That's mothers for you.

Maria We starting cooking a lot at home . . . Nobody cried when there were other people there, there were no unnecessary conversations . . . Like in a bloody war . . . (*Short pause*). And there were days when we all just started bawling . . .

Anna That's when we realised –

Maria That we were ready for anything.

A flash of light. The office. All the women are sitting.

Melissa . . . You are ready for any meeting at any level –

Tatiana With any audience.

Elena When do we leave?

Tatiana You leave in two days.

Olga And you?

Melissa The situation is a bit more complex for us . . . (*Short pause*) In as much as –

Elena I knew it.

Anna In what way?

Tatiana We can't go with you.

Maria You promised.

Tatiana Unfortunately, it's not up to us.

Melissa Don't worry – everything will go perfectly.

Elena Alone? We won't go alone!

Melissa You're not alone – you're together.

Elena No, it's out of the question. I don't know what everyone else feels but I won't go . . . We don't know anything . . . Where do we go? . . . Who do we talk to?

Melissa Actually, you're the people who know that best.

Olga And how will we explain everything when we're there?

Anna What about the translation?

Tatiana We've found an excellent interpreter – he'll help you for everything.

Maria That's a bit better . . .

Elena It's the loneliness . . . We're alone in everything . . . again we're alone . . .

A flash of light. Christmas.

Anna Alone . . . how many years . . .

Olga Seems like we've completely given up on today being Christmas . . .

Tatiana It's easy for us to remember but for them . . .

Maria Let's fill the emptiness with hope . . . Remember that woman from Columbia, she said: "to be a relative of an abducted person is to be filled with emptiness: emptiness in your heart, emptiness in your home, emptiness in the meaning of your life. It means you will remember every day . . . But life continues not only for yourself but for your children who need hope and truth."

Anna Do you think they see what we're doing?

Tatiana I don't doubt it.

Maria I was 14 at the time . . . They sent a young teacher to our school. All the girls were in love with him. He was completely different – not like the others. His classes in astronomy were outdoors. He showed us the stars . . . (*Pause*). Next year we would have had our silver anniversary.

Pause.

Maria When we had just got married, I went off on a business trip for a month and didn't call him once during that month. I didn't even think that I needed to call – nobody had taught me to do that. I didn't even think that someone would be worrying about me . . . He told me not to worry. Because he was taught that way . . . Taught to care for others . . . (*Pause*) At the end of our life together, he had taught me that, too. (*Pause*). Once I went for a training to Moscow . . . I'm walking around the town – it's grey, cold – and I understand that I'm so tired of this Moscow and so heavy, so sad, so miserable. And suddenly I had the thought that I wasn't alone, that I have a husband who loves me and I love him . . . I think: I should call him – and right away I felt better. I went to the post office, paid for a call, I call and he picks up the phone and asks: "Why are you calling?" I said: "I miss you," and he says: "A-ah, that's good". (*Pause*) Once he said to me: "I would be completely happy if you loved me half of the amount I love you". But I did love him. I said to him: "I love you so much. Why should I love you more? I just don't know another way of expressing my feelings and thoughts." It turns out you have to learn to love the people nearest to you. He taught me that, anyway . . . it's just that he's not with me anymore . . .

Anna I taught my husband that . . . I always said to him: "I love for us both: for you and for me".

A bright light. Maria sits on a chair in the middle of the stage.

Maria So that's how we live: for them and for us. (*Pause*). That journey which we got ready for, went ahead . . . After that, there were a few hundred more . . . and we keep doing them even now, until we've found out the truth . . . (*Pause*) From the moment my husband disappeared, and up to my life now, I've lived a whole life . . . And it is a much more serious and complicated life than the previous one . . . I've become completely different . . . (*Pause*) At first, there was only darkness around me . . . and horror. Horror that he wasn't next to me . . . . (*Short pause*). He wasn't next to me . . . and never will be . . . Only in my dreams.

Pause.

My husband was a very strong man. I never in my life saw his tears . . . I used to come home from work before, upset and crying. He would calm me down, and explain that to cry, you need a proper reason and there's no point crying for stupid little nothings. He was my support and my protector. A few months after his abduction, I saw him in my dreams . . . He said: "Save me" and tears were running down his cheeks. (*Pause*). They forced my husband to cry . . . (*Pause*). I became the way my husband wanted to see me: independent, responsible for myself, for my actions, for my life. Now I don't have anyone to hand over my responsibilities to or decisions. I must look after my inner life, after myself, so I don't go to pieces and don't turn into a nasty old witch. (*Pause*). I must answer for my family although my daughter is already an adult and each one has her own life but nevertheless, I'm an island which is ready to offer them shelter . . . (*Pause*). To realise all of that . . . I had to live through certain situations . . .

Anna comes out from the dark and sits on the chair next to Maria.

Anna The feeling of confusion is one of them . . . During our first journey, we were still a bit naïve, a little bit stupid. We didn't judge the auditorium, we didn't know our own strength and that was our weakness. But we were a team and we had the feeling of justice on our side. The trips around the world and the conversations with the high-and-mighty gave me hope that I will know the truth about the fate of my husband. Perhaps not tomorrow, not even in the near future, but I will find out . . . (*Pause*). The authorities don't like our movement. They'd prefer us to sit at home by ourselves and cry into the night . . . To mourn for our loved ones and blame anyone but the authorities . . . (*Pause*) I can't be weak now . . . I mustn't – I have a son . . . He's all that I've got: infinite love, responsibility, pain, joy . . . (*Pause*) This is the continuation of my husband, this is his reflection . . . Now he tells me he loves me. If an hour goes by without him saying something tender, it's wasted time for me . . . and for him . . . (*Pause*). And I also like that he tells me everything. Even how he kissed a girl at a club. So we're friends . . .

Elena comes out of the dark and sits down at a distance from Maria and Anna.

Elena My friends prepared everything for my trip . . . I can't live anymore in constant fear . . . Every time the doorbell or the telephone rings, I'm paralysed . . . I knew that even the slightest pressure on my children would kill me . . . My son is the spitting image of his father. My nearest and dearest stayed – they will always look after my husband's grave . . . (*Pause*). I took my children to Germany . . . I did that for them . . . and for their grandchildren . . . (*Pause*). At first it was very difficult . . . But now

it's easier . . . They're young and I don't have the energy any more
. . . But I can breathe here and I can walk down the street normally
. . . without fear . . .

Olga comes in and sits on a chair.

Olga Nothing is more frightening than a person's death . . .
especially someone close . . . And if he's abducted and killed . . .
and you know that you'll never see him again . . . I'm lucky . . .
very lucky . . . my husband is alive . . . He came out of jail and my
children have their father again . . . I stopped all my trips soon
after he got out – I wanted to make up for the time without him
. . . Although I know that with the current regime everything can
change in a day . . .

The light goes over to Maria.

Maria My life was broken in a second. I understand that what
we are doing should make something change. Even if I knew that
my actions wouldn't lead to anything, I would still carry on . . .
Because I can't quietly sit and watch them destroy my family. I
won't let anyone do that. Everything I've done in the last years
– it's a fight: a fight for the honour of my husband; a fight for the
peace of my family; a fight for the happiness of my children; a fight
for the health of my mother – because she's been helping me to
cope with this tragedy, she fell ill and can't get out of bed anymore;
a fight for my country and for myself. I don't want anyone else to
see the nightmares which I have.

THE END

TITYUS THE IRREPROACHABLE

by

Maksim Kurochkin

"Each year adds to the variety of our fruits
and the delightfulness of our flowers."

The World Set Free, H. G. Wells

THE EARTH'S SPIRIT

Having failed to spread effectively beyond the borders of the Solar System, Humankind froze in a pitiful, semi-exploded state. Many social institutes still functioned; many idealists could still be found discussing progress and God; absolutely healthy children were still being born now and again; spores of complex life were still being scattered into the distant cosmos. But the Earth's spirit – and a conglomeration of inhabited planets and planetoids continued to bear that name – was broken. Convicts awaited execution and, although each day of despair was followed by a new day, it did not give hope but only brought the inevitable closer. To replace humankind, what should have appeared bang on cue was a new dominant species . . . existing beyond the material realm, unreliant on steadfast moral systems.

Our species did not want to step aside without a fight. A Local Bureau was created for the fierce and hopeless fight against the future. But even the increasingly painstaking identification and destruction of post-human life forms could not stop the once neglected genesis. First at one end, then at the other end of the inhabited space, the feeble, variform but monumentally clever creatures appeared. They were engendered by illnesses; by medicines made to cure the illnesses; by artfully interweaving electronic sequences. They were engendered by the very eternity of the Universe which multiplied these manifestations of civilisation into an impressive panoply of colours. And the feebleness of these super-intelligent beings was not to last for long.

THE CAPTAIN SAID

The Captain of the Local Bureau was relatively healthy, almost illiterate, two small houses on the unflooded coast brought him an income equal to half of his monthly salary, which was a not inconsiderable sum. The Captain had two sons, a sheep dog and an Irregular Wife who was pregnant with a boy. The next ten years were promising . . . promising nothing. The world he lived in was not a place for promises.

The captain was dying to say it. And he said it . . . Bitch!

And that was the achievement of eight days of persistent effort using all of his spiritual and physical capabilities. Nobody else had succeeded in swearing in a semi-anabiotic state.

The captain was very angry at the stewardess who had forgotten her half-eaten sandwich in his capsule. With the constraints of a long flight, the smell of chicken can become a serious trial even for a trained killer.

INDIGENOUS POLICE

On Pluto, they were waiting for the captain.

White Man with Black Face Welcome to Pluto, sir.

Captain What's happened?

White Man with Black Face I'm afraid it's no longer relevant. We just received an order. They've recalled you.

Captain When is the return flight?

White Man with Black Face Straight away.

Captain Good luck.

White Man with Black Face Thank you. We'll deal with it.

The lock closes behind the captain.

White Man with Black Face At least, we'll give it our best shot.

On the return flight, a different stewardess is assigned to the capsule.

PROMOTION

Office of the Administrator-Killer

Administrator-Killer How was your outing?

Captain Good, thank you.

Administrator-Killer What's this story with the stewardess?

Captain I expressed myself in an improper fashion towards her.

Administrator-Killer Those whores often use the capsules as a fridge. They transport low-level contraband and food. I can imagine what you had to . . . Staying locked in one place for two weeks with boiled turkey. With no chance to move . . .

Captain It was chicken. A chicken sandwich. It felt as if two nails had been driven into my head, nails made of chicken.

Administrator-Killer Yes, strange things can happen with feelings in the capsules . . .

Captain They were thick nails. It was like they were being screwed in.

Administrator-Killer I sympathise.

Captain I shouldn't have sworn. But I didn't think it would influence my mission. I regret it turned out this way.

Administrator-Killer That's true, your action affected your return. But you don't have any cause for regret. Local specialists coped perfectly.

Captain I'm glad to hear it.

The administrator-killer is noticeably nervous.

Administrator-Killer How did you do that?

Captain Do what, sir?

Administrator-Killer Saying "bitch"? How did you do that?

Captain I was furious at her . . . She was smiling so sweetly when she closed the capsule . . .

Administrator-Killer Nobody else has managed to do what you've done. Not one other person has emitted a single sound in the capsule.

Captain I don't know. I was furious . . .

The administrator-killer gets out large sheets of paper.

Administrator-Killer Do you understand that you've achieved the impossible? This is a record of your mental activity. This is the point where you took the decision to call an employee of the "United Spaceways" a bitch.

Captain The point?

Administrator-Killer Let's put it this way: the phase of taking the decision ends here and a period of active realisation starts here.

Captain And what's the time scale?

Administrator-Killer Days. The phase of taking the decision took four days, the realisation phase – eight days. Look at the chart. It looks like the variance is insignificant. But if you take into account that it happened in a capsule of semi-anabiotic sleep . . . For eight days, you prepared your brain and body for this – I don't know what to call it – accomplishment. You're a very strong-willed man, Captain. We want to offer you a new job.

IRREGULAR WIFE

A room in the irregular wife's flat.

Irregular Wife Bella and Steve have invited us to their engagement on Friday.

Captain Each person goes mad in their own way.

Irregular Wife It's just an excuse to have a good time –

Captain I don't think so.

Irregular Wife You're a pain in the neck.

Captain Those ceremonies weren't a joke for our parents. They couldn't allow themselves to play at getting married every other week.

Irregular Wife We're only talking about an engagement. And they celebrate their engagement at most once a month.

Captain I don't like it.

The irregular wife is upset but tries not to show it.

Irregular Wife Bella looks so good in those dresses.

Captain Damn it, don't we have anything else to talk about?

Irregular Wife So what should we talk about? You never tell me anything about your work.

Captain They've offered me a promotion.

Irregular Wife That's great! Hardly anyone is being promoted these days. Now will you, finally, buy a real Chinese jeep? You need a good car.

Captain Don't you want to hear what work I'm doing?

Irregular Wife Isn't that secret?

Captain It's hard to believe, but no. For the first time in my life I'm doing work which isn't secret.

Irregular Wife That's wonderful!

Captain I don't think so. What's that smell?

Irregular Wife What will you be doing?

Captain I'll be . . . Will you come with me to the theatre?

Irregular Wife (*disappointed*) To the theatre?

Captain Yes, the theatre. the fucking cock-sucking theatre! What were you expecting to hear?

Irregular Wife Nothing.

Captain The theatre. Not the church. Not the town hall. The theatre. Just – the theatre. They're forcing me to go to the theatre now.

Irregular Wife I'll go with you. I'll go anywhere with you. Sit down at the table, the chicken's almost ready.

Captain Chicken?

Irregular Wife Mexican-style chicken.

Captain I need some fresh air. Don't worry. I'll come back.

THE TELEVISED DEBATE

Administrator-Killer . . . their capabilities surpassed human capabilities eighty years ago.

Optimist So what? As far as I can tell, I'm not yet controlled by an enemy's artificial intelligence.

Administrator-Killer Your mistake itself is telling. Yes, I agree that they don't control us *yet*. But that's because we prepared for those dangers. We mustn't forget for one second that there are beings, all around us, who are more intelligent than us.

Optimist Nor has there been a dangerous increase of man's biological capabilities. We're not being eaten by mutants, bat-men aren't flying in through the window.

Administrator-Killer And haven't you thought about why it's so quiet on the streets? Why teenagers fell silent? Why gangs make so little noise, why they've un-learnt how to speak? I can answer that. They send the command "give me your wallet" telepathically. You just don't want to notice that.

Optimist You need to update your scare-mongering stories. The last time I got my wallet out was thirty years ago when I was being filmed in a crowd scene for a historical film. You know perfectly well that my wallet, like everybody else watching us, is sewn into our skin and not accessible to thieves. And I ask you not to call me a cyborg, for that reason alone.

Administrator-Killer The implanted chip is not just a wallet, it's also a passport and a medical card, and an entertainment centre, and a note book . . . It's everything without which you can't exist.

Optimist You're right, people quickly get used to the good things in life. But the high quality of these services is a sufficient reason not to refuse them. Machines complete and strengthen my body. A computer strengthens my intellect . . .

Administrator-Killer We've not known for long time what computers are doing. One thing we know for sure: they periodically test the strength of our defences. We're still coping. So far.

Optimist And you'll keep coping – until you need a pay rise. All of this is too familiar: the medicines market shapes the illnesses market far more than the other way around. As soon as you don't have enough money, you think up a new danger –

Administrator-Killer You're right – there's not enough money.

Optimist My money – please note! I pay taxes and keep your gang afloat.

Administrator-Killer That's why you're alive.

Optimist That's why you aren't begging in the metro. Society is too tolerant towards people like you. That's why not a week goes by without screams in the newspapers about a new centre of super-intelligence . . .

Administrator-Killer The screams in the newspaper appear only once a week because the other six days a week, our people manage to detect the new centre before the journalists . . .

Optimist Tell me, what was the fuss about on Pluto? Why was it necessary to blow up a whole population, one house after the other, in order to destroy an unfortunate, frightened boy?

Administrator-Killer The first thing that the unfortunate, frightened boy tried to do, after admitting he was one of the super-intelligents, was – he tried to throw himself into a rubbish recycling system . . .

Optimist Funny! You built an abattoir out of a pile of rubbish.

Administrator-Killer Yes. To control rubbish recycling. But on Pluto there's nothing but rubbish recycling. The boy wanted to control everyone. And you can be sure – he wouldn't have stopped at Pluto.

Optimist Let's say it *was* like that. The question remains. Why was this necessary, important, timely operation carried out by simple police and militia? Why are there so many deaths? Where were your much praised agents?

Administrator-Killer The Local Bureau sent a representative to Pluto.

Optimist Was he late?

Administrator-Killer He arrived on time.

Optimist Then what was the problem.

Administrator-Killer We called him back. I'm afraid that's all I can say.

TOO OFTEN

Irregular Wife You come so often now . . .

Captain I can come the same amount as before.

Irregular Wife No, I like it when you come this often. I like it very much. When people want to see each other more often, that means –

Captain It doesn't mean anything.

Irregular Wife Of course, it doesn't mean anything.

The irregular wife tries to get offended. She almost manages.

Irregular Wife You find a second meaning in everything I say. Relax. I don't want to marry you. I have your children and I'll have more children with you. You gave me a lovely CD stand – what else do I need?

Captain Is that true, you really don't want to get married?

Irregular Wife You're an intense person. We see each other twice a week at the moment. That's quite enough.

Captain You mustn't be angry with me. This isn't an easy time for me.

Irregular Wife Don't you like your new job?

Captain I don't know . . . I can't understand it. I'm just reading.

Irregular Wife You're reading?

Captain Reading, I'm reading.

Irregular Wife That's cool! Have you read "Monster in the Aquapark"? Bella says it's amazing, on a level with "Micro-Jesus the Diver".

Captain No, it's too difficult for me. So far I've only read half the comic book about the raccoon-parachutist.

Irregular Wife Your new work is having a bad effect on you. Before, when you weren't reading, you were sort of . . . calmer.

Captain Before – . . . Yes, I was calmer.

Irregular Wife You were calmer before. But what did you do at work before?

Captain By the way, you didn't tell me how it all went with Steve and Bella.

Irregular Wife Wonderfully. She had a plunging dress in front, and here – a bouquet of live flowers. Steve also had a very nice suit. And in the evening he admitted that he was wearing a corset . . .

Captain A corset?

Irregular Wife In a real male corset. Can you imagine?

Captain Fantastic!

JUST A DOCTOR

Captain I've killed them in their homes, I've killed them in the cosmos, I've killed them under the ground . . . I've killed children, worms, nano-robots . . . I've burnt down planets which were covered in intelligent slime . . . I've used magnetic pincers to blow up balls of self-organising plasma . . . I killed a family of dolphins with a baseball bat. Have you ever killed dolphins with a baseball bat?

Doctor   Never. I'm just a doctor.

Captain   Why do I feel so bad?

Doctor   Are you experiencing any specific psychological difficulties?

Captain   Yes, you could say that.

Doctor   In the Peking zoo, a drunk Chinese man wanted to hug a panda. The panda bit him. Then the Chinese man . . . bit the panda.

Captain   I haven't heard about the mutant-pandas.

Doctor   No, the panda wasn't a mutant. Just a bear cub. But I want to talk about the Chinese man. Let's try to *feel our way through* the motivation of this gentleman. He's drunk, he's come to the zoo after a heavy week, he's filled with feeling towards the cute bear cub, it never even enters his head that the furry creature could turn out to be unfriendly. The drunk Chinese man – that's you and me. Because we're clearly not that panda. We clumsily try to embrace the world which seems inoffensive to us. And we get what we deserve – angry, painful bites. Yes, we deserve them. The naïve are always wrong. But we should learn from the Chinese man. Instead of justifying the world: "he doesn't understand, he's acting on instinct" . . . Instead of that . . . the Chinese man bites the panda. We are bound to answer a bite with a bite. Understand me, it's not a call for revenge. It's just there are two types of beings: furry, angry pandas and stupid drunk Chinese men – like us.

Captain   You haven't understood me. Once I took care of a thinking squirrel. She didn't represent any danger. But I had the order to destroy anything more intelligent than a cigarette lighter. And she was more intelligent than a cigarette lighter. I crushed her morally, I killed her physically, I destroyed her molecularly. There didn't remain even a single crumb-sized part of her DNA in the whole universe. I don't consider that to be right – to kill a thinking squirrel. And even at the time I didn't consider it to be right. But I killed her and felt good. Because I understood what I was doing. I understood what I had done. I kill intelligent squirrels. It's wrong . . . but I understand what I'm doing! And what am I doing now? Why do I need to read comics? I'm not interested in the adventures of the quilted balloon, I can't relate to him. I don't understand what's happening!

Doctor So you've already read about the raccoon-parachutist?

Captain Yes, I liked the story of the raccoon.

Doctor You'll also like the quilted balloon. Make sure you read it to the end. Try to understand the motives of his actions, analyse what's worrying him, what he loves, what he hates . . . When you finish, I'll give you Chekhov.

Captain You said I'd have to read Shakespeare.

Doctor All in good time. The quilted balloon. Chekhov. Agatha Christie. And then Shakespeare. Shakespeare – that won't be easy reading.

Captain I've heard that he's cool.

Doctor He's cool.

Captain But why all of this?

Doctor It's your work, officer. Either you do it or you suck cock.

Captain I'll do my work, sir.

He stands up to leave.

Doctor By the way, how did you like the theatre?

Captain The first production was . . . impressive. The second was . . . impressive.

Doctor Did you understand anything?

Captain No.

Doctor Fine, we'll discuss that next time.

THE DIAGRAM

Workers of the Local Bureau in the meeting room.

Administrator-Killer Look at the diagram. Who can explain to me why we're in the shit? Sean!

Analyst-Killer They're still appearing, sir.

Administrator-Killer Sean, even for an analyst, you're as thick as shit. No offense. But you really are as thick as shit. The problem is not that they're appearing. But that they have started to appear less often.

Intern-Killer Do you think they're planning something?

Administrator-Killer I don't know. I really don't know. But it frightens me that we're winning.

Analyst-Killer Our methods of monitoring are becoming more effective. We are managing to kick the ball straight into the net.

Administrator-Killer Sean, I don't like insulting people. So just don't say anything. (*He is noticeably worried.*) According to all our formulae, there should be more of these animals every day. Mathematics is against us. So why are we winning? We haven't stopped complicating the cosmos. And we're fighting against ourselves. So why are we winning? We grew tired and stopped believing. So why are we winning?

Intern-Killer They've thought something up.

Administrator-Killer I don't know. Maybe the truth is even worse.

Intern-Killer Can there really be something worse than a conspiracy of the super-intelligents?

Administrator-Killer The only thing worse than a conspiracy of super-intelligents is something for which we can't even think up a name . . . Just – *Something*. Or – *Nothing*.

Intern-Killer Very optimistic.

Administrator-Killer Optimists in our office clean the bogs. Paul, I, for some reason, immediately thought of you. How is the work moving forward with captain "Half-anabiotic Bitch"?

Doctor Captain "Stinking Sandwich" has finished reading the comic book "Quilted balloon and the tiger princess" and he's now reading "Quilted balloon and the mystery of the seventh asteroid".

Administrator-Killer Is there no way to speed up his preparation?

Doctor He's a slow reader.

Administrator-Killer The theatre?

Doctor He's already been to the theatre four times.

Administrator-Killer And?

Doctor He doesn't understand a thing.

Administrator-Killer I need him to understand and be able to analyse what he's watching.

Doctor He's trying.

Administrator-Killer If a man – who was able to swear in a condition of suspended death – is trying, he should succeed. You're not pushing him hard enough.

Doctor We're doing everything possible.

Administrator-Killer That's not that right answer. I don't have time. They're up to something. We need to start work on Monday.

Doctor That's impossible.

Administrator-Killer That's the right answer. But we *will* begin working on Monday. Have a good Friday. You're all dismissed.

CHICKEN AND RICE

Captain You see, in his childhood he made friends with artificial wadding. Then the law changed and his friend was made illegal. He hid for some time. But then they found him anyway.

Irregular Wife His friend?

Captain Yes. His friend. And when they wipe ketchup from their shoes with the synthetic balloon, the natural balloon swears to dedicate his life to the fight against injustice.

Irregular Wife The fight against genocide.

Captain Yes. He fights against genocide, he fights against gender-discriminatory crime, he educates the children of immigrants.

Irregular Wife You're so good at telling his story.

Captain I like it when I can discuss literature with you. It's very important – to feel that you're being listened to. The quilted balloon's not the most popular hero. Too few people understand him. But the people who manage to understand him are an elite.

Irregular Wife Are you still not eating chicken?

Captain I don't know . . . Maybe I'll try some. Chicken and what?

Irregular Wife Rice.

Captain Maybe I'll try some. (*Looks at his plate with chicken.*) No, sorry, I can't.

MONDAY

Captain But I only started reading Chekhov –

Doctor I'm afraid there's no time. They're pressuring us.

Captain I'm not ready –

Doctor You can never be completely ready for this.

Captain I don't understand anything. They walk around on stage – they say words. The audience laughs. Which means, they understand something. But I sit there and I don't understand anything.

Doctor It takes a certain strength to understand a contemporary play.

Captain I'm trying.

Doctor It's not enough for you to try. I'm in big trouble because of you. Soon I'll be cleaning the bogs because I believed in you.

The Administrator-Killer comes in.

Administrator-Killer Son. We need you.

Captain I'm not ready.

Administrator-Killer Nobody's rushing you. We're not hurrying anywhere. It's just that today we're slightly changing the programme.

Captain Okay.

Administrator-Killer You already know what a play is, don't you?

Captain Yes, sir. They're acted in the theatre. Actors play out a text in characters.

Administrator-Killer I know you've already seen a lot of plays.

Captain Not a lot. I've been to the theatre four times.

Administrator-Killer And you didn't understand a thing?

Captain I didn't understand a thing. I *felt* something –

Administrator-Killer If I wanted you to feel something, I'd order two boys to attack you with a cosh. One would beat your heels and the other would hit your balls. I'm not sending you to the theatre to *feel*. I'm sending you to the theatre to understand.

Captain I'm trying, sir.

Administrator-Killer So you can understand and explain to *me* – an old fool – what those fucked up contemporary playwrights are trying to say with their fucked up plays! So you can explain to me what *they* understand that I don't! . . . What they are warning me about, me – a man who has to warn others! Do you understand how important this is?!

Captain I'm trying, sir.

Administrator-Killer You're not trying enough, son. Anyway. I'm giving you a last chance. Today we won't watch contemporary plays. To hell with them. Now you'll watch a classic play . . . It's a very famous, old play. Written by Shakespeare. You know master Shakespeare?

Captain I've heard a lot about him.

The doctor wants to ask the Administrator-Killer something.

Administrator-Killer This is how it has to be, Doc. (*To the captain*) Listen to me carefully, son. It's a very famous, very old play. Clever people have written so many books about this play that you would need three of your lives just to read their table of contents . . . The master encoded his phenomenal predictions in this play. He showed humankind the dangers which we can't see. Son, I need you to understand this play and tell me what you understand. Do you understand?

Captain I understand.

Administrator-Killer I trust you. You are able to do this. If, of course, you *want* to.

Captain And if I don't manage?

Administrator-Killer You'll go back to tormenting speaking cats.

Captain Squirrels.

Administrator-Killer Squirrels. But you *will* succeed. Let's begin.

Workers of the Local Bureau enter. They settle down in the chairs. An actor comes out on stage.

Actor Tityus the Irreproachable.

Administrator-Killer A play by William Shakespeare.

Actor (*after a scarcely noticeably pause*) Tityus the Irreproachable. A play by William Shakespeare. The characters:

> Tityus the Irreproachable – the last military commander
>
> Suburbius – clerk by nature and fate, then General Bureaucrat of the Universes
>
> Architecton – General Bureaucrat of the Universes
>
> 1st Bureaucrat – cosmic bureaucrat

2nd Bureaucrat – cosmic bureaucrat

Pearl – wife of Suburbius, then . . .

Pork – wife and fool of Tityus

Bureaucrats of the Universes

Boy

Prophets – 10,000 prophets

Blob – unidentifiable physical phenomenon

Solid Citizen

Lucius, Papos, Mix, Concrete and 21 other handsome young men – sons of Tityus

'In the future everyone will be anonymous for 15 minutes.'

Robert Banks

Administrator-Killer (*to the doctor*) Who's this Robert Banks?

Doctor Nobody knows.

THE PARTY

The dining room in the building of the United Humanities. A private evening event of the Supreme Bureaucrats to mark the victory of Tityus in the last war and the final ending of all wars.

Architecton A fine speech, Suburbius. But Tityus's merits which you mentioned about are but a fifth of his merits, the rest of which you passed over in silence.

Suburbius But it was only a fifth of my speech. I stopped to gather my strength for the remaining four fifths, which exceeds the first fifth, much as the strength of four giants exceeds the strength of one dwarf.

Tityus Well, if the dwarf is already that good, it's not worth troubling his older brothers.

Architecton Tityus, is it really unpleasant for you to hear about the man who stopped violence across the inhabited cosmos?

Tityus If his name weren't Tityus, I'd listen until my ears were whittled down by praise.

Architecton But he is called Tityus and it's *you*.

Tityus Tityus is a loud word.

Architecton Aren't you happy that you're Tityus?

Tityus Neither happy, nor sad.

Architecton The answer is worthy of the name Tityus even if Tityus isn't worthy of his name.

Turning to all who are present.

Today, I have decided to leave my post of General Bureaucrat of the Universes. Years of ordeals and struggles have not made me stoop – but they have made my soul go stale and my tongue has almost been torn up lengthways. So the high post doesn't suffer any harm, the time has come to yield power to someone more deserving.

Suburbius We know that the General Bureaucrat weighs his decisions painstakingly. That is why, though mourning his premature retirement, we must hastily consider a successor.

Everyone Tityus! Tityus!

Architecton Do you hear that, Tityus? The United Universes shout your name.

Tityus The United Universes should have a good think before bawling at the top of their voices.

Architecton I recognise your way of expressing yourself, stern Tityus. But, when I referred to a successor, I also meant you.

Tityus I ended one hundred wars and prevented another fifty from starting. I'm not old, I can work without sleep, my strength only increases with every new threat. When I am at the office – and I'm always at the office – the enemies of the Humanities never dare to lift their heads. I have brought peace to nations that were at war since Adam. I have fed planets that could not gulp down enough food since the invention of the spoon. Children are given my name in three hundred and seventeen of the three hundred and eighteen inhabited universes. And this is the person you want to give the authority to: General Bureaucrat of the Universes? Where's your reason, your caution, where's your understanding of Man – so boasted about by our age? Have you really forgotten the lessons of our history? Who'll vouch that I won't turn into my own contradiction and start launching wars on the pretext of their final eradication? Who's measured my arrogance and anxiety? Who knows the strength of my fears and the depth of my shame? Me –gaining the power of the Supreme Bureaucrat? Me – whose irreproachability is crying out about his mania? Me – the artful diplomat and powerful strategist? Me – who has spent his youthful years in the most terrifying jails on the planet of jails? Me – who suffered a thousand violations? Me – lifted from the depths, retaining all the habits and manners of the lowlifes? Me – to be given political power? You've gone out of your minds.

Architecton I didn't expect a different answer from the gracious Tityus.

Suburbius Alas, we're forced to judge the thoughts and intentions of people only by what the security cameras see. But all the actions of each person, from the first cry to their last minute are monitored. Don't worry, Tityus, we have amplified each of your smiles to the size of a football pitch to be certain that there are no hidden threats in them. All of your secret glances, your shouts in the night have been studied and described by scientists no less than the structure of amoeba. We know everything. There is nothing to reproach you with, Tityus!

Tityus *There* is the best proof of our vulnerability! You checked my actions, my words and gestures. You know which side I sleep on, how I clean my nails, which hand I use to button my trousers. But if you could glance into the basement of my secret dreams . . . You'd find locked boxes with secret compartments.

Architecton The law of the United Spaces protects the freedom and inviolability of thought as the greatest value. Man doesn't have responsibility for his visions.

Tityus Visions wipe out more people than all the deaths taken together and multiplied by themselves.

First Bureaucrat Tityus, we respect you as a specialist in threats to Humankinds but you're not strong in mathematics.

Tityus When I talk about visions which kill, I don't just mean the nightmares of tyrants which end in genocides. People worry about lavishly sowing the seeds of life, fearing dark shadows . . . I'm talking about those not yet born.

Second Bureaucrat But you've defeated similar fears. Twenty-five sons is not a bad result for the big league.

Tityus I'm proud of my sons. And I mourn the four who died cleaning the world of violence.

Suburbius We won't speak about that now . . . Tityus said the arguments against Tityus but he still hasn't removed his candidacy.

Tityus What do you think, Suburbius?

Suburbius Yes, I think the matter should proceed thus. In order not to waste time, I suggest voting. Who is for Tityus taking the post of Supreme Bureaucrat?

The bureaucrats vote mentally.

Suburbius Tityus, you are elected in the name of Humankinds!

Tityus O, the carefree! Tityus is too treacherous to believe his self-abasement, too great to increase his power, too proud to be satisfied. So this is my first and last decision as Supreme Bureaucrat: I voluntarily relinquish this post and ask the Council to elect as its head a man unremarkable for his valour or intellect. A man who shall not enflame the heart with speculative rhetoric, who is poor on audacious intentions and too anaemic to become a usurper. I ask you to elect as Supreme Bureaucrat a work-loving mouse, a diligent pygmy, a biped carbon-copy of an official . . . I propose Suburbius!

Suburbius Me?

First Bureaucrat Who is in favour of Suburbius occupying the post of General Bureaucrat of the United Humankinds?

The bureaucrats vote mentally.

First Bureaucrat Suburbius, you are elected in the name of Humankinds!

Tityus I am pleased but I don't congratulate you, Suburbius. Your election is our general shame.

Suburbius And I thank you, Tityus. If not for your inhuman severity towards yourself . . . If you didn't value your talents so highly and had not taken so much into account my . . . I had not the slightest chance of ruling the worlds. Well . . . By tradition, a General Bureaucrat who has voluntarily left his post receives a large reward – the right to an absolutely private life. Nobody living has what you two will receive today.

Tityus I don't need rewards. I fulfilled my duty less than a minute.

Suburbius Thirty-four and a half seconds.

Tityus And I didn't resign it for the reward.

Suburbius Who, other than you, can know the truth?

Tityus Observation does not interfere with my personal life.

Suburbius Allow me not to believe you in that, Tityus. We all acknowledge that the swarm of microscopic spy-cameras which circle around us is a necessary measure. Humankinds sorrowfully deprived man of his right to solitude. But there's no other way. Each of us is too dangerous. Only complete monitoring holds our species back from the brink of destruction. Only the fear of immediate exposure restrains inimical intellects from attacking. But if we could avoid that, if a method could be found of living without a loss of freedom-

Tityus No need for lectures, Suburbius! You know perfectly well that I myself did everything so that every child in the very furthest corner of Spaces is met at his birth by a personal swarm of flying eyes. With tears in my eyes, I sowed spying-eyes across all the earths, even the empty ones. And the grief of any earth which refused to take my grain . . . It met its dawns in blood. It washed myself in blood at night. With fire and the sword I quietened those who stood against my non-violence. The salvation of our race I see in the hated spying-eyes. I'll not deceive you. I don't think that my life will change after I'm no longer followed.

Suburbius Whether your life changes or not, that can only worry you and you alone. You're on a pension, Tityus, and you can give yourself up to contemplation. We don't have time. Bring in the cups.

Two cups are brought in.

Suburbius Worthy Architecton and Tityus! For the first time, two Supreme Bureaucrats drink this code at once. Drink it and live a long life, free from immodest glances.

Architecton and Tityus drink from the cups. The Cosmic Bureaucrats congratulate them.

Architecton Tityus, a word . . .

Architecton and Tityus step aside from the Bureaucrats who continue to make merry.

Architecton Tityus, you're an ass's prick. Why did you need to retire?

Tityus I told you why – I'm afraid of myself.

Architecton Stop talking rubbish. Nobody is listening to us now.

Tityus But I am genuinely afraid of occupying such a high post.

Architecton Tityus! I waited two hundred years for the moment when I can talk without worrying whether my words will be used against me . . . And you, Tityus, you are the first person I'm talking to . . . how could you . . . You – who even before never feared to speak openly . . . Why continue this shameful game of loyalty? We've done our time, we've earned the right to lampoon and curse everything which oppressed and controlled us for so many years. We gave a lot of strength to the thing we wanted to believe in, now we're on a pension, we are finally free . . . We can walk around our flats naked and scratch our grey balls as much as we want, read enemy books, wipe our arses with the symbols of the United

Humankinds . . . Can you imagine, there's only two of us . . . In the whole worlds . . . Only two absolutely free citizens.

Tityus I am surprised by the change in you. Do you mean, you were not yourself, all of this time?

Architecton Either you have a plan or the Pope had your mother. Well, if you don't want to be open with me, you don't have to. But know this, that by opening the path to Suburbius, you strengthened envy and greyness, brought to nothing all of my efforts to hand power to someone worthy. I know Suburbius – he will take revenge on you.

Tityus What reason could Suburbius have for taking revenge on me? He's untalented and a coward. And I gave him power.

Architecton For that exact reason, that's why he'll take revenge.

Tityus I hope, along with your responsibilities, you relinquished your gift of telling the future.

Architecton It's a shame that's not so.

Tityus We're being called.

Architecton Ah, Pearl's arrived, Suburbius's wife! She's found out about the big change in her husband's fate. She's an attractive little chicken. I've been glancing over at her for a long time.

Architecton and Tityus return to their colleagues.

Architecton Hi Pearl!

Pearl Hello, General . . . (*laughs*) Hi Ton!

Architecton and Pearl exchange greeting kisses.

Architecton I want to introduce you to Tityus.

Pearl So you are the madman my husband is obliged to, for his unexpected promotion?

Tityus Everything your husband has is thanks to him alone.

Suburbius Colleagues! Citizens! I will leave you for a short while. I beg you to forgive my weakness – I want to show my wife my new office. Let's go, Pearl.

Pearl (*to Tityus*) Pleased to have met you. I hope we'll see each other more often.

Tityus I don't think so. I was planning to leave the central universes and spend the rest of my days in the outskirts.

Pearl Will you be healing your wounds?

Tityus I'll be learning to drink whisky.

Pearl Good luck!

Pearl and Suburbius go off into the office of the General Bureaucrat.

Architecton I know why he called her over and dragged her into the office –

Tityus I'm not interested.

Architecton They won't make love there, they're going to talk.

Tityus Haven't they talked for a long time?

Architecton I think they've never talked like THAT. There's a cubicle for secret discussions in the General Bureaucrat's office. He can't take his wife in there on a normal day. But today is a public holiday and they let her into the building. I understand him all too well. I remember how I dragged my old girl in there on the very first day . . .

Tityus My sons have arrived. Concrete, Papos, Lucius . . . How many of you are there?

Lucius We all came – to congratulate you.

Tityus hugs Lucius. All of Tityus's sons come in.

THE CUBICLE

Suburbius and Pearl in the cubicle. Pearl sits on her husband's knees.

Pearl It's very cramped in here.

Suburbius This cubicle is only designed for one person. General Bureaucrats hold their secret discussions with the Local Bureau from here.

Pearl Will you also have those kinds of discussions?

Suburbius This is not the time for trifles.

Pearl Look, the spying-eyes have fallen asleep and they're lying on the floor like dead flies. I've never seen that.

Suburbius What were you talking about with Tityus?

Pearl Can't you look at our conversation yourself?

Suburbius That's the thing, I can't. His image and voice are no longer being recorded.

Pearl I've never had to tell someone what I was talking about . . . But I'll try. First, I called him mad –

Suburbius No, no. He's anything but mad. That beetle knows what he's doing.

Pearl He said he's not involved with your flight to the top.

Suburbius Don't believe that lying animal.

Pearl My God, you're talking so funny. I like it a lot. Why do we never talk like that at home?

Suburbius We'll talk like that at home someday. If I retire voluntarily, I will be invisible to the observation cameras, like Tityus is now. And then – I promise you – I'll talk *only* that way, and even funnier . . .

Pearl But I don't want you to retire. I always dreamed of being the wife of a General Bureaucrat.

Suburbius I'm also not planning to leave my post. He's just waiting for that –

Pearl Who?

Suburbius Tityus. I've sussed him out. His affected nobility is a cover for plans so monstrous that even in here, where nobody is listening to us, I can't bring myself to say my suppositions out loud.

Pearl He wants to start a new war?

Suburbius Why a war? He gets more by protecting the peace. Pilgrimages will spring up, there's no doubt about it, like the ones to the holy men . . .

Pearl He said that he's not planning to stay in the capital. He's moving to the outskirts.

Suburbius Of course. He wants to work out who he can rely on. His most faithful allies won't hesitate to fly across the universe to reach him.

Pearl My God you're clever.

Suburbius I'm clever, Pearl. Remember that when I'm saying stupid things. I will tear up Tityus's plans and, if it comes to it, I'll destroy his treacherous kind. If only you knew how he dared to humiliate me.

Pearl Humiliate my rabbit?

Suburbius Don't call me your rabbit. Never.

Pearl But you like it.

Suburbius growls strangely.

Pearl Fine, I understand.

Suburbius And also . . . When . . . When . . . Well, after . . . You understand?

Pearl I don't understand.

Suburbius After we . . . together.

Pearl Together?

Suburbius Damn! Every time, after we've fucked, you fiddle with my hair.

Pearl Yes, I like fiddling with your hair. And you always smile when I do that.

Suburbius Don't EVER do that again.

Pearl But you like it.

Suburbius NEVER DO THAT AGAIN.

From outside, the shouts of a large crowd can be heard: "Suburbius! Suburbius!"

A Bureaucrat of the Universe tears into the office.

Bureaucrat of the Universe Ten thousand and one prophets have gathered on the square. They want to talk to you.

Suburbius There's no mistake? Exactly ten thousand?

Bureaucrat of the Universe There's no mistake. They've prepared well.

Suburbius (*to his wife*) We have to go. They've fulfilled the constitutional prophetic minimum.

Pearl For some reason, I feel scared, Ubi.

Suburbius Pearl, it's shameful to fear charlatans.

THE SQUARE

The square in front of the building of the United Humanities. A ten-thousand strong crowd of blind prophets. Suburbius comes out to the crowd.

Suburbius I have been informed that the blindmen are holding a meeting on the square.

Prophets Yes, that is so.

Suburbius According to the constitution, I am obliged to listen.

Prophets We are ten thousand and one blindmen.

Suburbius I am the new General Bureaucrat. I am listening to you.

Prophets (*together*) Save Suburbius, while there's still time.

Suburbius Is that all?

Prophets Save Suburbius, while there's still time.

Suburbius I take care of my personal safety least of all. Go! All of you!

Prophets (*together, especially powerful and frightening*) Save Suburbius, while there's still time.

Pearl I'm very scared.

Suburbius I'm calling out the water-cannons.

The square in front of the United Humankinds empties in an instant.

Suburbius They didn't take their time in gathering a crowd to scare the General Bureaucrat. But I only had to mention the water-cannons and they disappeared off the face of the earth. In fact, I wouldn't have used any water-cannons on my first day in the new post.

The prophets instantaneously fill up the square again.

Suburbius The normalising gas – that's what the madmen should respect.

The square empties again instantaneously.

Tityus A bitter but exact observation. Maybe I was mistaken and you, Suburbius, are not at all the fool you seem to be.

Suburbius Not a fool, correct –

Tityus Maybe it was not a good idea for you to become the General Bureaucrat.

Suburbius Who knows?

Architecton How do you intend to act upon that prediction? It cannot be ignored, it is writ in the law.

Suburbius I'm afraid I didn't catch the question.

Architecton How do you intend to act upon that prediction? It cannot be ignored, it is writ in the law.

Suburbius Say that again, I didn't hear it.

Architecton (*shouting*) How do you intend to act upon that prediction? It cannot be ignored, it is writ in the law.

Suburbius I still can't hear you.

Architecton Ow, damn, he's mocking me.

Tityus I got that right away.

Architecton How unpleasant. And nothing to prove it. Our words can't be heard.

Tityus But we have witnesses.

Architecton Witnesses were excluded from legal proceedings long ago. Who needs testimony from imperfect people when there is data from perfect machines.

Tityus Respected Suburbius, do you not think that you are acting impolitely towards your predecessor?

Suburbius Hey, guards, check the square. I think that the blind men left behind lots of vermin.

Architecton Treachery.

Suburbius Were you afraid? (*He laughs.*) Well, old men, am I able to dissemble?

Tityus I was ready to swear that you were serious.

Suburbius Dear friends, I will always answer any of your questions, the doors of my house are always open to you.

Architecton Even my heart started hurting.

Suburbius The very time to have a little drink. (*He invites all the guests into the building with a wide gesture.*) Please.

❧ *INTERVAL* ❧

Administrator-Killer Stop! Thank you. Five minutes interval.

Doctor (*to the captain*) Will you go for a smoke?

Captain No, I want to think.

Doctor As you wish.

Some colleagues, including the captain, stay in their seats. Some leave to smoke and drink water.

Doctor Maybe it wasn't a good idea to tell him it's Shakespeare.

Administrator-Killer Why?

Doctor He'll guess it's a lie.

Administrator-Killer How?

Doctor Shakespeare couldn't have written such drivel.

Administrator-Killer But he doesn't know that.

Analyst-Killer It's drivel of the rarest kind.

Doctor I didn't understand a thing, if I'm honest.

Analyst-Killer It's not possible to understand. It's a contemporary play.

Intern-Killer That joke was funny.

Analyst-Killer Which one?

Intern-Killer I can't remember.

Administrator-Killer Right, lads, final round.

Colleagues of the Local Bureau return to their seats.

Administrator-Killer We can continue.

The actors continue the play about Tityus the Irreproachable.

THE FOOL AND CHILDREN

Tityus returns home.

Tityus Where are you, fool?

Pork Your wife cooked dinner for the whole family plus pensioner.

Tityus I bought nothing. The electronic checkout sees neither me nor my cards.

Pork Good you have children who care about you. You are insured against starvation twenty-five-fold.

Tityus It still feels unpleasant to lose my money. True I haven't built up any capital but what's important is the principle. You know, I never thought there could be consequences like this.

Pork Sit down, I've prepared some pork.

Tityus Pork has cooked pork.

Pork Your wife has made lovely pork chops.

Tityus I don't like that you call yourself my wife. We agreed. You've been my fool for the last ten years. Have you really forgotten that?

Pork People don't sleep with their fools. And you slept with me last month and in March and in February –

Tityus Would it suit you better if I get a new wife?

Pork A fool that prefers to be slept with. By the way, they say you cut off your male particularities today.

Tityus Who told you that stupidity?

Pork Your son.

Tityus Which one?

Pork Every son who came into the kitchen to see me, to steal a spare rib or to drink some milk.

Tityus All of my sons spoke in the same manner?

Pork All except the dead ones. The dead ones don't have that possibility.

Tityus Gather my sons. I want to talk to them.

Pork It's not the fool's job to organise family councils.

Tityus Pretend that it's your new joke.

Pork Poor fool who doesn't feel the slightest inclination for tom-foolery.

Tityus Listen, I'm fed up of your whining. Even yesterday I was ready to put up with it because I didn't have time to take care of you. But now I'm on a pension and I want to dot all the "i"s.

Pork I better go and call our sons.

Tityus Not yet, first we will resolve all of our issues.

Pork All of them?

Tityus If I conquered violence in the whole world, can I really not conquer –

Pork Your wife?

Tityus What's "wife" got to do with it? I asked you not to call yourself that.

Pork I forgot again. I'm a fool.

Tityus Yes, you're a fool. If you don't like your duty, you can go to hell. (*He sees her tears*) Pork, my darling, don't cry, I don't mean to hurt you. Sit down, let's talk.

Pork sits down next to Tityus. They sit down like infinitely distant people.

Tityus We've been married for one hundred and thirty years. We married when I was twenty and you were nineteen. I loved your smile, your walk, your words about people and the world, your tears, shyness, courage, breasts, your birthmarks, legs, source of your legs, your backside, your morning caprices, for thirty years I satisfied your wishes, for thirty years I studied your . . . For another thirty years, we gave birth to children. But, Pork, my darling, let's admit the obvious . . . For the last forty years, we can't fulfil the rituals characteristic of couples without sniggering. When I touch you, you don't feel anything except tickling. When I see your naked boy, I become bored like in chemistry class as a child. Nobody can bear so many years together . . .

Pork Do you want to divorce me?

Tityus Undoubtedly that would be the right thing to do. All of our acquaintances divorce automatically after eighty years of marriage. Something about us is not right. It's hard for me to divorce you.

Pork Something about us is not right.

Tityus But anyway, it was a bad idea – to let you play the fool.

Pork But it's my only way of staying with you.

Tityus Yes, it's the only way of keeping you beside me. But you are not fulfilling your promise not to remind me of the past.

Pork It's hard. I was happy with you.

Tityus Of course, it's hard. You know, sometimes even for me, looking at you, I remember our best one hundred years. But you think that it's easy for me to go around without a woman at my age?

Pork For that reason, you have a fool.

Tityus It's not right – to sleep with a fool.

Pork But nobody can reproach you if you . . . From today, your personal life is untouchable.

Tityus And it's *you* saying that? Do you consider that this laughable privilege will change anything about me? I'm Tityus. I'm too proud not to do anything out of fear that it will be found out. And too fastidious to make use of the possibility of not being punished. It makes no difference to me – let all the eyes of the world watch me. I won't change.

Pork That's exactly the point, nobody is watching you anymore.

Tityus I am my own best spy. There is no code which could force me to stop spying on Tityus. "Tityus lives without a wife but when it becomes completely unbearable – he sleeps with his own fool!" I'm fed up of these reproaches.

Pork Who would dare to reproach you?

Tityus Tityus. Who else's reproaches would I fear?

Pork Fine. If you are suffering so much: *I'll* leave *you*.

Tityus Pork, don't say such stupid things. (*Embraces his wife.*) How would we manage without each other?

Pork You can be so rude.

Tityus   Pork, everything's in the past . . . Let's just live. Where are the children?

Enter Lucius, Mix and another twenty-two sons of Tityus.

Pork   What happened? Where's Papos?

Lucius   Our brother was arrested.

Tityus   What did he do?

Lucius   Why didn't you ask "what is he accused of"?

Tityus   Who are you to teach me? If your brother has been arrested, it means he broke the law.

Lucius   Father, our brother isn't guilty of anything.

Tityus   How can you say that?

Lucius   Because I know my brother as well as myself.

Tityus   You know what I did in the cosmoses with people who broke the law?

Lucius   Father, don't forget that I'm your military general. I fulfilled the toughest of your orders and I remember that not once did I doubt in their justice. But if your order had aroused any doubts in me, I would have submitted myself.

Tityus   And you remember that all of my tough but fair orders were given not in my name but in the name of the United Humankinds?

Lucius   That means something bad has happened at the United Humankinds –

Tityus   I can sooner believe that Papos betrayed the ideals of non-violence.

All of Tityus's sons   That's impossible.

Papos enters. Pork throws herself at her son. She embraces him.

Pork   Papos. You frightened me.

Papos   Everything's good, mama. What have we got for dinner?

Pork   I'll bring in the pork chops now.

Pork leaves.

Tityus When do you have to go back?

Papos I've been let out for one hour.

Papos embraces his brothers.

Tityus It's time for you to go back, I don't want you to be late.

Lucius Won't you even embrace your son?

Tityus When you atone for your guilt before the United Humankinds, I'll be the first to embrace him.

Papos Farewell, Tityus.

Tityus Farewell.

Lucius Papos, tell us one thing – what's the reason for your arrest?

Papos Suburbius.

Papos leaves.

Lucius It's inhuman.

Tityus Who do you plan to teach humanity?

Lucius You. You're an old maniac, Tityus. I'm pleased you didn't become the Supreme Bureaucrat.

Tityus That only proves I was right. Remember, Lucius, your father is never wrong.

Lucius I used to think that, too.

Pork comes in with the pork chops.

Pork Where's Papos?

Lucius Mama, he'll come back soon.

Pork Did he come to say goodbye?

Lucius Everything will be cleared up soon and they'll let him go.

Tityus Don't listen to him, Pork. Papos is guilty and will be punished.

Pork It's impossible. My boy could never do anything against the United Humankinds.

Tityus Don't make me laugh. You're squealing "impossible" as if you're becoming hysterical. And I don't want to have a fool who gets hysterical.

Mix Father. She's not a fool. She's our mother.

Tityus You, boy, do you plan to teach me?

Mix You're not leaving me a choice.

Tityus I'll explain to you what it means not to have a choice. Do you see this? If you want me to take your words seriously, you know what to do.

Tityus shows Mix the knife.

Mix Father, you've got it wrong.

Pork No!

Mix directs the knife in Tityus's hand into his own chest. He dies.

Lucius What have you done, Tityus?

Tityus Who else wants to teach me?

Lucius (*to his brothers*) Brothers, our father has gone out of his mind. But he'll repent when he comes back to his senses. Let this be the last victim of his madness.

Tityus Do you dare to accuse me of your brother's demise?

Lucius Silence, brothers. Look to our mother.

The brothers carry out the unconscious Pork.

Tityus And you, go.

Lucius Father. I believe that you are mad. I'll submit to you.

Lucius leaves.

Tityus Dangerous boy. If I had my way, I wouldn't let anyone under ninety open their mouths. He imagined I have a plan which demands such a thorough camouflage, it needs me to kill my own children. But is there any aim in the world which demands such a sacrifice? (*Thinks.*) A stupid question. Who hasn't sacrificed their sons? Only the lazy. If one thinks about it, caviar are just slimy balls. Small change – that's what children are. It's stupid to cry if it falls out of your pocket. But Mix! Mix!! How I loved that boy!

Enter Lucius.

Lucius Father, there's news. Your son, your Papos who you didn't want to embrace or guard against false and dangerous accusations –

Tityus What, son?

Lucius Papos is guilty. The judges said that.

Tityus Guilty – then he's no longer a son of mine.

Lucius Guilty and he confessed under the weight of the evidence.

Tityus Guilty and he confessed? No, he's not my son.

Lucius Guilty and he confessed. And to avoid any violence, he waded voluntarily into the eternal ice.

Tityus Voluntarily? So that he wouldn't break the principle of non-violence. He's mine! My son! My poor Papos!

Lucius Oh, if I could talk freely, without the fear of being heard by others –

Tityus Why did this happen? Come. You're protected from curious bees if I embrace you.

Lucius comes close to Tityus.

Tityus But if you use this cover to tell the truth, you're no longer a son of mine.

Lucius (*stopping*) I don't understand. But I already hate it.

Lucius leaves. Blob appears.

Tityus Today, I conquered violence in all worlds, ruled Humankinds for a few seconds, lost all my money, lost two of my sons, one of whom I killed with my own hands . . . And now I'm having strange visions. Who are you, Blob?

Blob I don't have any memory. I only just gained consciousness in this room.

Tityus Maybe you are the spirit of my dead son?

Blob Did you have a son?

Tityus I had a son. I had sons. I have sons. Which son am I talking about? But maybe you're the general soul of all of my boys who have perished? The world is full of mysteries and why not allow that souls can merge together like broken eggs in a frying pan?

Blob You're idea seems convincing to me.

Tityus So, you're able to reason. What other abilities do you possess?

Blob I think reason is the mother of all abilities. He who can reason can do whatever he wants. So I don't know all of my abilities but I think I have as many as there are abilities in the world: despicable and virtuous.

Tityus Yes, you're a philosopher. Comfort me. Nobody wants to comfort me. My fool refuses to be like proper fools.

Blob So his ambitions exceeded his duties.

Tityus Let's say that's how it is. Then how can he achieve the most if he can't cope with the least?

Blob That's how he will achieve it. The only path upwards is not to cope with what you've been given.

Tityus How did I achieve everything?

Blob And what did you achieve?

Tityus I'll tell you without boasting that today I was head of all the Humankinds for thirty-four seconds.

Blob Thirty-four seconds isn't so little.

Tityus Exactly.

Blob And how long did your predecessor hold onto the post for?

Tityus Around two hundred years.

Blob That's not so much if you think about it.

Tityus Blob, stay with me. You'll be a comfort to me.

Blob One can't comfort a person who's looking not to be comforted –

Tityus What am I looking for, according to you?

Blob I'm just a Blob. I can only make a conclusion based on facts.

Tityus Which facts do you need?

Blob Who are you, what do you fear, what do you want?

Tityus I am Tityus. Friends and enemies without agreeing on it gave me the nickname "The Irreproachable". I'm not afraid of anything. It's truer to say I'm afraid of only one thing – I'm afraid of being afraid. I want . . . I don't want anything any else. I want to live the rest of my years in peace.

Blob I'm only a trembling Blob who recently gained consciousness. But even I understand that everything except your name is a lie.

Tityus Well, well . . . You think the same way as my favourite son Lucius. He's also sure that I have a plan exceeding all previously known conspiracies in scale and treachery. He's convinced that my humility is posture. That my self-restraint has the opposite aim to its purported purpose.

Blob If I knew what empathy is, I would say that *his* thoughts are close to mine.

Tityus Petty. You're petty. You can't believe that a man can put limits on his own strength.

Blob But you must agree, the history of Humankinds confirms *our* suspicions sooner than your sworn beliefs.

Tityus I'm above swearing.

Blob You see . . . you won't even swear to it.

Tityus Don't joke with me.

Blob Who's joking . . . ?

Enter Pork.

Pork Well, my friend, have you found a new pastime?

Tityus Rather a secretary. Let me introduce you, Pork this is Blob, Blob this is Pork, my fool.

Blob Pleased to meet you.

Pork I can't say the same.

Tityus Blob, you mustn't be offended by my fool. She's had a difficult time, today.

Pork True. I'm on my feet since morning. Preparing pork chops for a large family – that's not so easy.

Tityus You forgot to say that two of your sons died today.

Pork Yes? I actually forgot. The main thing is my master didn't drive me away.

Tityus Pork, come here, I'm going to give you a hug.

Pork No. He who hugs a fool, never becomes what he wishes to become . . .

Tityus What do I want to become?

Pork You know.

Tityus Pork, why the jokes? You know I don't like that.

Pork Really? Why do you need a fool then if you don't like jokes?

Tityus You remember what nickname I had before I married you?

Pork They called you Tityus the Just then.

Blob Why did you lose that nickname?

Tityus There is a universal justice in the fact that I got Pork. But nobody could call me just anymore because there's no human justice in the best person getting the best morsel. So I stopped being Just and became merely Irreproachable.

Blob A sad story. But it seems your train of thought has gone off the rails.

Tityus An Irreproachable's thinking can speed up and slow down. But never go off the rails. Even if people don't consider me "Just", I still stand in front of eternity, to them. And there's no humiliation worse than when you're suspected of something which you didn't commit.

Pork That's right. You're innocent of whatever people suspect you of. Since they're only intentions.

Tityus What intentions, Pork? Today I've already been leader of all Humankinds. What else could exceed that power?

Enter Suburbius. All (including Tityus) go down onto one knee.

Suburbius (*making a sign for them to stand up*) I see nothing will calm you down?

Tityus I don't understand – what are you talking about?

Suburbius Your sons have been seen doubting and whispering secretly. Their fists are clenched, their teeth grate, their eyes roll around their sockets . . . All the signs point towards their dissatisfaction with the carriage of justice.

Tityus What has their father got to do with it?

Suburbius What has their father got to do with it? A funny question.

Tityus What has their father got to do with it if their father is Tityus? You know that I could not compel – either in word or deed – my sons to doubt the justice of the current system of justice.

Suburbius How can you prove what you say?

Tityus You know that I didn't take on the name "The Irreproachable" to allow myself to be reproached on secret activities to the detriment of Humankinds.

Suburbius How can you prove what you say?

Tityus I refused to embrace my son who was accused of doubts and whispering. I non-violently killed my other son, who accused me of not embracing my son who was accused of doubting and whispering. I refused to give my third son the opportunity of expressing his secret thoughts . . . Is that not enough?

Suburbius It's enough for me to name you as a general enemy of Humankinds. It's a real pity that I won't be able to prove your actions in a court.

Tityus Here is my fool. Here is my secretary. They will confirm every word of mine.

Suburbius I only see your wife and a blob of an unidentifiable physical nature.

Pork I'm not a wife. I'm a fool.

Blob I'm not a Blob now. I'm a secretary.

Tityus Secretary, call in my puppies.

Blob Puppies!

Tityus's sons appear.

Lucius You called us?

Tityus You are the festering wound of my old age. How could you allow my home to become a hot-bed of violence?

Lucius Father. None of us is mixed up in violence.

Tityus Isn't it enough that you're breathing more than usual? Is it so hard to see: it's only the lack of murders which is stopping you from becoming murderers?

Lucius Shame colours our cheeks. But we are true to the ideals of peace.

Tityus Why then does the General Bureaucrat accuse you of betraying those ideals?

Lucius Father. Can you really not see that Suburbius hates you and everything you achieved on this earth? He is the opposite of Tityus. Everywhere there's a lot of you, there's not much of him. Where you are wide, he is just needles. His soul is less than a stapler and he can only compete in nobility with a second-hand dealer of viruses. You still have twenty-three sons . . . And Suburbius could not even engender a worm. When you brought non-violence to whole galaxies, he was opening bottles of beer at the Bureaucrats' meetings. Now he wants to eradicate the slightest memory of your doings, soil you with the dirt of suspicions.

Tityus Even if everything you said were true . . . how can you dare to forget his high office?

Lucius Only respect for the system of Cosmic Bureaucracy keeps us from sharp words and actions.

Suburbius So you see, Tityus. What other proofs of betrayal are needed?

Tityus Wild beasts! Bastards! How can you dare to be accused of being enemies!

Lucius Open your eyes, Tityus. You have no reason to reproach us or yourself! Nothing can be proved against us.

Tityus "Tityus The Irreproachable" – not because they can't prove anything but because he's irreproachable. And all of his emissions should also be irreproachable.

Lucius We're not Tityus's emissions. We're people. We can make mistakes. But even a blind man would see that there's no truth in Suburbius's accusations – there's only his hatred to everything which reminds him of Tityus.

Suburbius Strong words which require proof.

Tityus I repeat after the General Bureaucrat. Strong words which require proof.

Lucius tears out his eyes. Suburbius feels unwell. Lucius reaches out his hands with his eyes to Tityus, thinking that it's Suburbius.

Lucius Here, Suburbius, take these bubbles. Even without them I can see what presents the real danger to Humankinds. Take them as the first payment for the tower of human flesh which you have decided to build.

Pork Son, you are stretching out your eyes to your father.

Lucius That's not possible. Has my heart really gone blind?

Tityus I'll take your eyes and hang them on my uniform. Alongside the most esteemed rewards.

He puts his son's eyes on his uniform.

Tityus Now I can say that never in all Humankinds was there an award higher than that which is fastened to my marshal's uniform of the 1st non-violent army.

Suburbius You're a herd of animals. You should be wiped out.

Pork You see, Lucius. Your sacrifice was in vain. Suburbius isn't satisfied.

Concrete We'll avenge you, Lucius.

Tityus What did I hear? Who dares to talk about revenge in my presence? Away from me, traitors. Get out, all of you. I can't let a caveman's morals come into the world through the doors of my home.

Concrete Are you driving us into the street, Tityus?

Tityus Yes, and immediately. Get out, all of you. Get out. My fool and Blob can stay.

The brothers leave, except for Lucius.

Pork (*to Tityus*) At least let Lucius stay. Where will he go without eyes?

Tityus None of my sons will stay. I've made up my mind. They're all stained.

Pork At least wait until his brain has stopped bleeding.

Tityus Pork, this is the second time today I'm making this observation – you aren't managing well with the role of fool. You should see off this blind man with kicks, by pinching him, by spitting on his head and tripping him up. If you don't change, I will have to think of you as one of them. I will also drive you out.

Pork I'll change.

Pork hits Lucius with all of her strength. He falls.

Pork (*to Lucius*) Why are you scrunching up your face as if you've eaten something sour? Seems like you don't know what sour really means.

Pork cuts a lemon in half and squeezes the juice into Lucius's eye sockets. Lucius shouts.

Pork By all means shout, go on shout. Maybe someone will guess what you're feeling now.

Tityus That's better, fool. But I didn't really mean you should torture him.

Pork Don't you see he likes it? He's entertained us wonderfully and for that we can return his eyes.

Tityus Are you suggesting that I return the award which I've been honoured with?

Pork Why? He needs something simpler. Anything will do. Even this.

Pork puts into Lucius's eye sockets the halves of the squeezed out lemons.

Pork Look, Tityus, he's flawless again.

Suburbius Your fool knows how to make some wonderful jokes. Where did the fool learn that sense of humour?

Pork Wandering behind the 1st non-violent army, you learn other things too.

Suburbius I feel that there's a lot left to find out about you, Tityus.

Tityus I wasn't pretending that battles on the edge of the cosmoses weren't hard. The time for my methods has passed. I didn't let myself take the high post so that the barbarity which I personify will remain in the past and the United Humankinds will at least sleep peacefully.

Suburbius While you're alive, the United Humankinds won't have a single peaceful moment.

Tityus What do you want from me, Suburbius? I drive away all my sons. I'm an old man. Without strength or an army. What do you want from me?

Suburbius I want you to come forward openly as an overt enemy of Humankinds. As long as you hide your true intentions, everyone will think that it's me who brought down misfortune upon your head.

Blob Aren't you asking too much from human nature? You'll find few who don't link Tityus's misfortune with your actions.

Tityus There's only one person who can judge that. That's Tityus. And I'm happy that I wasn't mistaken about Suburbius. Not a single enemy of Humanities will slip unnoticed past this rabid dog. And my misfortunes don't trouble me much.

Lucius Save Suburbius while there's still time!

Suburbius (*to Tityus*) You know what your allies are saying now? They're saying that Tityus never used to be so hard-hearted.

Tityus I was.

Suburbius They maintain that you're suffering gravely, acting unjustly with your sons.

Tityus It was as difficult for me to drive away those animals as wiping my arse.

Suburbius Your allies are convinced that your bravery has been rewarded with dirty ingratitude. They consider that you didn't deserve my suspicions and criticisms.

Tityus You're only doing what everyone would have to do, in your situation.

Suburbius But your allies, who are increasing by the minute, are convinced that the non-entity Suburbius is avenging his humiliation on the greatest hero of the last war.

Tityus Only you and I know that they are not right.

Suburbius But the more you approve my actions, the larger the number of people who sympathise with you. Only a few more and there will be an insurrection against the power of the Supreme Bureaucracy.

Tityus What should I do to avert the blood-shed?

Suburbius Tell them honestly about your true intentions. Call your allies to the fight to overthrow the existing order . . . Only then will they believe that you are a wolf in sheep's clothing.

Tityus I am a wolf in demon's clothing and a demon in wolf's clothing. Put me in jail on a chain – that's the least you should do.

Suburbius How could I put you in jail on a chain? There are no witnesses against you. You are irreproachably leading the world to catastrophe.

Tityus Tityus The Irreproachable – that's exactly what they call me.

Suburbius Oh God, if only you knew how much I hate you!

Blob Do you remember that each of your words is heard in all of the inhabited cosmoses?

Suburbius Yes, my words are heard! But not his.

Blob Tityus shouldn't be reproached. Everything he says respects the spirit and the letter of the general precept of non-violence.

Suburbius Tityus, take care!

Blob You understand – that was a direct threat and it was officially recorded by all the observation cameras?

Suburbius Good-bye, Tityus. I'm going to prepare the water-cannons and the normalising gas. I'll fight.

Lucius Save Suburbius, while there's still time!

Suburbius puts his hand on Lucius's neck. He looks into his lemon-eyes. He leaves.

Pork He's a terrifying man. He's gone.

Lucius I'm dying, father.

Tityus People don't die in our day and age from the wounds you have.

Lucius I think that Suburbius, before leaving, crushed my carotid artery. I'm losing my strength. Good-bye, Tityus. Good-bye, Pork.

Pork Son!

Lucius Mama!

Lucius dies. Pork cries over his body.

Tityus I don't want to accuse Suburbius until his guilt is proven. I'm far from thinking that he would go as far as murder. More likely, Lucius's heart broke from foreboding. But in any case, I see that Suburbius is too afraid of my sons.

Blob You can understand why.

Tityus You can understand why. Fly to my sons whom I drove away. Tell them I'm ordering them to voluntarily give themselves up to the authority the General Bureaucrat.

Pork And if he decides to make them wade voluntarily into the eternal ice?

Tityus Then, that must be. I don't plan to give in to doubts about his right to act that way.

Pork But they're your sons! Your sons, unfeeling Tityus!

Tityus Who said "unfeeling"? Is that you, my fool?

Pork Me, their mother.

Tityus (*to Blob*) How can you accuse me of not having any feeling, the woman who made a thousand attacks on my feelings? Are you still here?

Blob Does the order to your sons remain as it was? It's not a mistake?

Tityus Have you really not understand even now that Tityus The Irreproachable never makes a mistake?

Blob disappears.

Pork I don't know you, Tityus!

Tityus You didn't want to know me, Pork.

Enter a Solid Citizen.

Solid Citizen Tityus, Suburbius sent me to you.

Pork What does that bloodsucker want?

Tityus What does the Supreme Bureaucrat want?

Solid Citizen Firstly, he asked me to say that your sons made clear their guilt in their cries of despair, their curses and their moaning. And they willingly waded into the eternal ice.

Pork Oh, grief!

Tityus What else?

Solid Citizen Suburbius asked me to say that most of Humankinds sympathise with Tityus. He asked me to find out whether you want to say something to your allies?

Tityus Neither in word, nor in deed, nor with the batting of my eyelids, will I give them hope that I approve their decision. What else did Suburbius ask you to say?

Solid Citizen He said that if you refuse to lead an uprising against him, he will be forced to resort to the final means . . .

Tityus Which one?

Solid Citizen Before I answer, please let me say several words on my own behalf –

Tityus Speak.

Solid Citizen Suburbius is besieged in the building of the United Humankinds. A bit longer and the crowd will break into the hall of celebratory sittings. And they will tear Suburbius apart.

Tityus What caused such hatred among the crowd?

Solid Citizen The order which Suburbius gave me and which became immediately known to everyone, for the General Bureaucrat, like any mortal except you and Architecton, is surrounded by spying-eyes.

Tityus What was the order?

Solid Citizen Before I answer, promise me that your anger will not fall on me. I am only the messenger. I am the last person who remains true to Suburbius.

Tityus Then I am your twin brother. There is no order from the Supreme Bureaucrat which I wouldn't accept with humility and respect.

Solid Citizen In truth, you are Tityus the Irreproachable!

Tityus So what is the Supreme Bureaucrat's order?

Solid Citizen Suburbius understands that he's lost. The weight of his visible but imaginary injustices has broken the patience of Humankinds. Before being shamefully overthrown, Suburbius decided to complete one authentic act of villainy. He considers that it is his last chance to stop you.

Tityus What is that act of villainy?

Solid Citizen He ordered me to kill your fool.

Tityus No! Not that!

The solid citizen gets out a gun and before Tityus can stop him, kills Pork. Tityus cries.

Tityus Suburbius! What have you done! I was faithful to you till the end. I forgave you the death of all my sons. But now I'm going to have to leave my home.

Solid Citizen You promised not to kill me.

Tityus I'm not strong enough to keep my promise.

Tityus kills the solid citizen.

Tityus Tityus the Irreproachable is no longer Irreproachable. It's over. Suburbius, you've got what you wanted, I'm coming to kill you.

ARCHITECTON

Weakened by hunger, Tityus lies by the locked front door of his house. Architecton goes over to him with a boy. Next to Tityus is the faithful Blob.

Architecton Look, son, there lies Tityus, the founder of peace in the habitable cosmoses.

Boy We were told about him in school. Why is he lying in the street?

Architecton He can't get into his house. The electronic locks don't see him and there's no-one at home to open the door for him.

Boy And why's he so thin?

Architecton He can't buy himself food. The electronic checkouts can't see him. That's why he's dying.

Boy Is he being punished?

Architecton No. Although there are things he could be punished for. He killed two people, one of them was the Supreme Bureaucrat.

Boy Like you, dad?

Architecton Like me.

Boy Then why didn't they make him wade voluntarily into the eternal ice?

Architecton They couldn't prove his guilt. You see, he's invisible to the observation cameras.

Tityus tries to lift himself up.

Tityus Blob, I want to eat.

Blob You've already eaten me a hundred and fifty times. But it's useless. I come out unchanged and I don't fill you up.

Tityus I want to eat you anyway.

Tityus eats Blob. Blob comes out of Tityus unchanged.

Tityus I'm dying. Architecton, is that you?

Architecton It's me, Tityus.

Tityus I can't get into my home.

Architecton There's no-one to open up to you. All of your sons are dead.

Tityus Suburbius tricked me. He lured me out of my home.

Architecton I can't imagine how he managed to trick you. You had worked everything out.

Tityus I worked everything out. My plan was so near to completion.

Architecton But he killed your wife.

Tityus I would have forgiven him for killing my wife. But he killed my fool!

Architecton You didn't take into account that you couldn't forgive the murder of your fool.

Tityus I didn't take that into account.

Architecton You regret that you couldn't enjoy simultaneously both the power of the Supreme Bureaucrat and the right to an absolutely private life?

Tityus I regret. I was close.

Architecton You were close.

Tityus You were luckier than me. You were elected again as the Supreme Bureaucrat.

Architecton Yes. And, I must say, to be unpunished by the government of Humankinds is a lot more pleasant.

Tityus You did what I couldn't do.

Architecton I did what Suburbius didn't let you do.

Tityus Suburbius was a great man.

Architecton Suburbius was only a photocopy. True, he had a fine wife.

Tityus What are you trying to say?

Architecton Good-bye, Tityus. Even if cameras aren't spying on me, I still can't resolve to say that truth.

Tityus (*shouts fearfully*) Architecton!

Tityus dies.

Boy Has he died?

Architecton Yes, son.

Boy But can *you* also die of hunger? 'Cos the electronic checkouts and the electronic locks can't see you either?

Architecton No, I won't die.

Boy Why?

Architecton Because I have you . . . and your mum.

Enter Pearl.

Pearl Boys, time for dinner!

CRISIS DISCUSSION

The Actor who read the list of characters enters.

Actor That's all. The play's over.

Nobody applauds.

Administrator-Killer It would be the right thing to do for us to thank the remarkable actors for their work.

The workers of the Local Bureau obediently clap. The actors bow and leave.

Administrator-Killer Five minutes break. Then discussion.

Some workers go out into the corridor. The captain remains seated.

Analyst-Killer Why did he need twenty-five sons? Two would be enough.

Intern-Killer Maximum three.

Analyst-Killer Maximum three.

Doctor What's the point of the play?

Analyst-Killer There was no point. The playwright is a total idiot. However, I did catch up on some sleep.

Analyst-Killer I think the author was trying to say that we're being spied on.

Administrator-Killer Sean, shut up!

Intern-Killer Poor Shakespeare. He's probably turning in his grave.

Administrator-Killer Does anyone else have an opinion?

Doctor I'm afraid not.

Administrator-Killer Let's continue.

The workers return to their seats.

Administrator-Killer Captain, your turn to speak.

Captain It was . . . impressive.

Administrator-Killer Tell us about the play.

Captain I'm moved to bits.

Administrator-Killer We're all moved.

Captain Shakespeare is an outstanding master.

Administrator-Killer Shakespeare is an outstanding master. Can you say something more specific? Did you understand the play?

Captain I . . . It's just . . . I . . .

Administrator-Killer Captain, answer one question.

Captain Yes, sir!

Administrator-Killer Did you try to understand the play?

Captain Yes, sir! I really tried to understand the play.

And it's clear that he really tried to understand it.

Administrator-Killer Then why, god damn it, didn't you understand it?! What stopped you from understanding this simple, age-old play?! (*He turns to those present.*) I mean – is it, a complicated play?

Analyst-Killer As simple as a chair.

Doctor A play for teenagers.

Analyst-Killer My little son knows it all by heart.

Administrator-Killer (*to the captain*) Did you hear that? I have come to the conclusion that you didn't sufficiently want to understand it!

Captain I really wanted to.

Administrator-Killer Then what the hell?!

Captain (*almost crying*) I don't know, sir. I'm so sorry. I will write a report recommending it for translation to perform for the mounted police.

Administrator-Killer (*calming down*) Get a hold of yourself. No report is necessary. I'm giving you two days to come to your senses. That's all. You're all dismissed.

Captain Thank you, sir.

The captain leaves.

Analyst-Killer A complete dead-end!

Doctor I don't think so.

Analyst-Killer Captain Rotten Chicken.

Administrator-Killer Sean. If you open your mouth without permission again, I'll kill you.

This sounds very convincing coming from the mouth of the Administrator-Killer.

JUST A WIFE

Irregular Wife How did it all go?

Captain A complete failure! They're saying to understand, I just have to *really* want to understand. But I don't think so. I really wanted to understand the play but clearly the desire alone isn't enough. Probably you have to watch very many plays, to study in special schools, to read critical articles, to take part in discussions . . .

Irregular Wife What was the play about?

Captain You see, Pork –

Irregular Wife What did you call me?

It's as if the captain didn't hear his irregular wife.

Captain The play is about the next five billion years when the Earth is not in danger of collision with other galaxies. For eight million years, we needn't worry about serious changes in the stability of the Sun –

Irregular Wife Is that what the play was about?

Captain That's all I understood.

Irregular Wife Shakespeare wrote about the stability of the Sun?

Captain Can you imagine how mighty he was! Hundreds of years ago, he foresaw that humankind as a race wasn't threatened by armies of insurgent machines or harmful alien life-forms. He considered that military viruses could not cause eradication on the scale of the Solar System. He saw that subatomic fires would burn whole planets but could not break civilisation. A simple lad from Stratford foresaw a time when friendly technologies would tie the hands of enemies. And humankind would have only one enemy left. And that enemy is . . .

Irregular Wife Who?

Captain I'm worried that you're listening to me so seriously.

Irregular Wife I always listen to you seriously.

Captain You understand . . . I'm just a stupid worker of the Local Bureau. What I understood is one hundredth of what well-prepared audiences understood.

Irregular Wife Answer my question . . . !

Voice of the Administrator-Killer Son, answer your irregular wife's question immediately.

Captain By the way, I've been wanting to ask her to become my regular wife. My darling, you won't object?

Regular Wife I won't object.

Captain Our main enemy . . . I can borrow the corset from Steve.

Voice of the Administrator-Killer Who is our main enemy?

Captain Were you eavesdropping on us, sir?

Voice of the Administrator-Killer Son, you're very stupid.

Captain I know, sir.

Voice of the Administrator-Killer But if you say who we should be afraid of, I'll forgive you everything.

Captain I can only tell you what I understood.

Voice of the Administrator-Killer Oh for fuck's sake, tell me quickly!

THE END

TECHNIQUES OF BREATHING IN AN AIRLOCKED SPACE

by

Natalia Moshina

PART I

Nadia

Vitya

A park in the hospital grounds. An alley, a bench. Nadia sits on the bench, with a book in her hands. Vitya comes over from the right, sits at a distance to her, on the very edge of the bench. They sit silently – a girl and a boy. On her, a wide-brimmed panama hat is pulled down low, on him – a bandana.

He sits and thinks that the girl is similar to one of the actresses who's always in the soap operas (although he doesn't watch the soaps), there's something about her – she's just like one of the actresses; there's something in common – but he can't remember which actress – he has a bad memory for names, and even faces are somehow blurred, he remembers them as a blur, a total blur, though he's seen that actress more than once, more than twice – her photo is often in the papers, and in the magazines. In other words, she's one popular actress. And this girl here is a little bit like her. No doubt about it.

And she sits and reads, and thinks that don Rumat was one heck of a bloke, devilishly handsome, but it's bound to turn out that he won't get there in time again, and the little Hugo will be killed – and each time you hope he'll be there in time, so they won't kill him . . . And she also wonders whether she'll cry again – she cries each time she's reads it; so it's probably better to get up and go over to another bench because something made this odd beetle land beside her, does he want to get to know her or something? Horrible . . .

But he finally decides to say something, understanding that it's all nonsense, of course, but anyway. He mustn't just sit like an idiot.

And he can't think of what to say for a long time and he sighs when he thinks of something. Such a load of old codswallop . . .

Vitya What are you reading? (*She, looking at him, silently shows him the cover.*) O-oh! "It's hard being a God".

Nadia (*without so much as looking at her conversant, returns to her reading*) Hm.

Vitya (*after a pause*) What, have you never read it?

Nadia (*after a long pause*) (I've) read it. (I'm) re-reading it.

Vitya Why?

Nadia (*turning, looks at him carefully*) I like it.

Vitya I reckon it's better to read something you haven't read before.

Nadia Why?

Vitya To find out about something else. Something new.

Nadia It doesn't bother me. I've lived enough. Thank God for everything I've had.

Vitya You're strange.

Nadia Listen, buddy, you don't want to move to another bench, do you?

Vitya No.

Nadia No?

Vitya Uh-huh . . .

Nadia Huh? Okay, fine. Then I'll move. (*She gets up awkwardly, he grabs her arm.*) Hey!

Vitya Please stay. I just wanted . . .

Nadia Yes?

Vitya To chat to you.

Nadia Why?

Vitya You look like an actress.

Nadia Me? Like an actress?

Vitya From the soap operas.

Nadia The Brazilian ones?

Vitya Please sit down. Stay here. (*And she does sit down.*) You're definitely not an actress?

Nadia Me? No.

Vitya No . . . ? Huh, I really thought . . . Are you sure you're not an actress?

Nadia Listen, sod off.

Vitya It's just I know you're so proud.

Nadia Am I? And how would you know?

Vitya You're always alone. I've seen. I've observed.

Nadia Haven't you got anything better to do?

Vitya It's lonely here.

Nadia Well, it's not a circus.

Vitya I know. But still . . .

Nadia (*after a pause*) How long have you been here?

Vitya A month. And you?

Nadia Do you find it difficult?

Vitya Well, yes, I suppose so. More than anything, it's lonely. There's no-one to chat to.

Nadia And that's why you came over and crash-landed by me?

Vitya Well . . .

Nadia To chat?

Vitya Have you been here for long, please?

Nadia What difference does it make? Is that really what you want to chat about?

Vitya No. I wanted to know your name. If that's alright, please.

Nadia Stop being so polite.

Vitya Fine.

Nadia Just relax. Look, do you want to chat me up or not?

Vitya Yes, I do.

Nadia Well, there you are, then.

Vitya (*after a pause*) It's groovy weather, isn't it?

Nadia Oh, boy, you're hard work. (*Stands up.*) Good-bye. Chat to the bench.

Vitya Hey . . . hey hang on! (*He shouts after Nadia, who leaves, without making any attempt to get up and chase her.*) Listen, um, I won't talk about the weather anymore!

Nadia stops, looks at him for a short while, then goes back and sits down.

Nadia I don't like talking to strangers. I don't like talking in general.

Vitya I've noticed that. (*Pause.*) Why are you here?

Nadia silently bends her head to one side, prods herself somewhere beneath the ear. Vitya carefully touches it.

Whoa. That's huge. What have you got? Lymphatic knots?

Nadia Uh-huh. And I'll bet you've got leukaemia. (*Vitya laughs and nods.*) I can always spot you guys a mile off!

They sit for some time silently, occasionally throwing glances at each other.

Nadia How are you about it? Fine?

Vitya Couldn't care less.

Nadia I see.

Vitya What's your name?

Nadia Nadia. Hope.

Vitya Beautiful . . . and I'm Vitya. Victor.

Nadia Victory.

Vitya Well, yes. Naturally.

PART TWO

Timofei

Kilt

Venya

Sveta

(All are students in their twenties.)

A room. Timofei, Kilt, Venya and Sveta sits in a semi-circle. All have sheets of paper in their hands, covered in writing, and notebooks.

Timofei Right, come on then, who's got what? (*He opens his notebook, the others shuffle their papers. A pause. He looks everyone over.*) Why's everyone gone quiet? What have you got? Come on . . . (*Pause.*) What is this? Hasn't anyone got a damn thing or are we too shy to start?

Kilt So what have *you* got, then?

Timofei (*he shakes his notebook*) *I* have something. I've always got everything. I'm interested in your results. Well? . . .

Kilt Well, you can start.

Sveta So?

Timofei Okay, the usual story. It's always me.

Venya And then us.

Timofei So, you do actually have something?

Kilt Oh yeah.

Venya We've been racking our brains for a week.

Sveta So?

Timofei Have we got anything good?

Kilt Fuck only knows. Start and we'll find.

Timofei Fine, damn the lot of you. Fine. H-hm. (*He clears his throat, looks at the notebook.*) Basically, here's the main idea . . . H-hm. First of all . . . Well, first – the main thing. H-hm.

Kilt You're pissing me off. Get on with it.

Sveta Well?

Timofei H-hm. Basically. Something like ecumenism.

Venya Wh-what?

Kilt A synthesis of religions.

Timofei Yes. A single God. Not Jehova, not Allah, not God-the father, in other words, just – God. Sort of a different One. A new One. Well, an old one of course, but nobody's kind of talked about Him before. A sort of Moses, Christ, Mohammed – they've all been banging on about another one, about another God. But the real one – that's Him. He's so genuine that all those prophets are like – He doesn't give a damn, He's just straight into a person's heart – hop-la! Without any intermediaries, know what I mean? I.e., you're sort of living when – g-bam! – and you feel Him: that's it, God's in your heart. Well, and then the rest.

Kilt Like what?

Sveta Well?

Timofei Well, and we'll like, gather them up, in the glory of this new God.

Kilt So there are intermediaries after all?

Sveta Well?

Timofei No-o! We'll be just, you know, the first to see the light.

Venya Ah . . .

Kilt And then what? How about the money?

Timofei Well, we can collect money, you know, for building a shrine to this new God. Along the lines of, old shrines are no good, because that was all a lie.

Venya And what's the whole thing going to be called then?

Timofei Ha! I thought of that, too: "The True God".

Kilt That's shit.

Sveta Hey . . .

Timofei Why?

Kilt But what's the idea? The task was to think up some cool new idea, some great con, so people immediately take notice and run for whatever it is to give us their money. And what have we got? "The True God"! It's backwards, that's a fact.

Sveta Yeah.

Timofei Okay. Okay. You don't like it – then fuck you. Come on, Kilt, we're listening to you, since you're so clever. We're ready to admire your idea.

Kilt Why are you getting so upset?

Timofei Come on, give us yours. We're all listening.

Pause. Kilt shuffles his papers.

Kilt 'Morons and motorways'.

Venya You wh-at?!

Timofei I knew it.

Sveta laughs.

Kilt Silence children! That was the working title: "Morons and motorways". The subtitle is: "How to rebuild Russia". The title and the subtitle can be changed later, what's important is the idea.

Venya Smells of politics.

Kilt Venya, Venchik, any religion is to some degree politics, and vice versa. Do you follow my thinking?

Venya Well, more or less.

Kilt So listen and be quiet. Anyway, the main idea is this. Everyone lives shittily in Russia but everyone wants to live well. To start living well, you'd need to sort out a load of shortcomings which make you live shittily. The main shortcomings were pointed out a long time ago, I can't remember which classic it was, but that's beside the point. The shortcomings were simple: idiots and roads – morons and motorways. It follows that if you eradicate the morons and the crappy motorways, living would become, at least to some degree better and even more cheerful. That's a fact, no?

Sveta And?

Timofei I'm digging this.

Venya Well, I like it. Really, I like it.

Kilt Thank you, Venchik. Who doesn't get what?

Timofei I don't get any of it! What morons are we talking about here, and what motorways? Well, let's say there *is* a problem with them, fair enough. But how are you suggesting we tackle it? And what's it got to do with a new religion? What's the basic idea? Where's the money going to come from?!

Kilt O-oh, that's easy. It will, naturally, require a lot of preparatory work but then the investment will pay off.

Timofei So what is it, what?

Kilt A secret religious sect! A huge, branching out, organisation, with a defined structure . . . actually, fuck the structure, the main thing is that we're at the top of it, all the money goes to us, and the rest are underneath us and they bring us the money. Hop-la!

Timofei Shit, man, what've the morons got to do with it? And the motorways? What's the idea, for crying out loud?!

Kilt To eradicate them, I already made that clear, no?

A thick pause hangs in the air.

Timofei Right.

Venya In other words . . .

Kilt Huh?! Powerful, no?

Timofei Right.

Venya I don't get it.

Sveta Kilt's in his element.

Kilt Ha!

Timofei Right.

Venya Sorry, how do you mean – "eradicate"?

Kilt Physically.

Venya Kill them?

Kilt Well, something like that.

Sveta "Something like that" or kill them?

Kilt Think about it.

Venya But how can you kill a motorway?

Kilt Blow it to fuck. Destroy it. So it's not there.

Venya Why?

Sveta So it's not there.

Venya They're already crappy, if you blow them up into the bargain . . . Well then . . .

Kilt And instead of the ruined ones, they can build good ones. We'll put out press releases to the media: it's like this, we're going to fight for the destruction of all bad roads to the very end. Until they build good ones.

Pause.

Venya Well, it has to be said, I mean, it's an idea . . . Blowing up the motorways . . .

Sveta Well yeah.

Timofei Right.

Kilt So, no questions or objections to the destruction of morons?

Pause.

Sveta W-well . . .

Venya But how . . . I mean, what will actually happen? Well, in terms of destroying them? I mean . . .

Kilt I mean, destruction.

Timofei Parameters.

Kilt Oh, Timson, I respect you, seriously. You always see to the heart of the matter. Well, you've got to agree, it's a good point!

Timofei Parameters.

Sveta What are you on about?

Kilt Our Timofei wants to know what parameters will be used to identify a person as an idiot, resulting in their destruction.

Sveta A-ah.

Venya There could be some exams . . .

Kilt There could.

Sveta And there could be some sort of observation . . .

Kilt There could.

Venya You could just start with all of the people with Down syndrome.

Kilt Easily.

Pause.

Venya Yeah . . .

Timofei It's still not a religion.

Kilt Actually, no.

Timofei Well, what were you thinking? The exercise was; think up a new religion which will help to bring money to its creators, according to the words of Hubbard that "if you want to become a millionaire, think up a new religion". Remember?

Kilt Yes, I remember.

Timofei Well, then, what are you beating yourself up for? Over rubbish like that . . .

Kilt You know, it's easy to make this work. We can think of it as a religious sect! We sit down, write a manifesto, pull out some quotes from the Bible, all pointing to the same thing: the existence of morons and shitty motorways are not worthy of the Holy Father. Easy as that. Shall we begin?

Timofei I don't know . . .

Sveta Timson is just envious.

Timofei Don't you want to have a go, darling Svetlana? Go on, show us what you wrote.

Sveta Oh . . . I had really only one idea: collecting money maybe for building a monastery or shrine, and then running off with it. (*The blokes laugh.*) Well, what are you smirking at? I don't know, I couldn't think of anything.

Venya That's really a sin.

Sveta What's a sin?

Venya "Building a shrine and then stealing the money"?

Sveta Yes? And killing people with Down syndrome?

Pause.

Timofei Okay, Venka, let's hear yours.

Venya I suggest a primitive cult based on neurolinguistic programming. A totalitarian sect, pure and simple. They'll bring us the money, no questions asked.

Timofei Yes? But what's original about that?

Venya W-well . . . Well, a collection of money for organising the Second Coming. A sort of – party, to build the temple again . . .

Sveta Ha! A party!

Kilt Uh-huh.

Sveta Cognac, caviar . . .

Kilt Naked girls dancing . . .

Sveta Ha!

Venya (*laughing*) Hey, shut it.

Timofei So, anyway, what have we got? Apart from the super-creative from Kilt, there's also my idea, which is actually more-or-less decent. It's better than Venka's or yours, Svetik.

Sveta Well, of course.

Timofei Yes, of course. What are you suggesting: can you imagine taking an economics exam with nonsense like that? "Collecting for a shrine or something, and then running off with the money"! The teacher would go nuts. As it is, he'll say that you can't expect anything worthwhile from us PR-people, and now he'll definitely say that. Are you saying "no"? Gentlemen, our future profession is to brainwash people in a literate way, to send them to the very place that they didn't think they would go a moment earlier! No, but it's true, isn't it? And we can't even think up some stinking new religion! Shame on us, dammit. Alright, I suggest we merge Kilt's and my idea, to make one super-idea, but we need to think it through. The test's the day after tomorrow, we're pressed for time, wakey-wakey!

Venya We know, okay.

Their heads bend together, a discussion begins. Timofei stands up and walks out to the front of the stage.

Timofei God? It's not about God. It's about a new religion. It's not even about an economics test. It's about the fact that, if Kilt is talking like an idiot, thinking up his secret terrorist sect, then it must be in the air. It must mean the thing I'm taking part in, this whole adventure, is, well, really meant to be. Yes. It proves it's all correct. The time has blossomed. True, there's a danger that the conspiracy will go to hell, because Kilt thought up something similar, then someone else will think it up, then another person, and then, dammit, the whole thing will get to the secret services. . . . Who will stop it though? The secret services? Can they really stop anti-government and anti-state activity? That's pretty funny. No, it's a good thing. Otherwise, three years of preparation, of the whole conspiracy – what's it all been for? And for me it's three years, but when did it actually begin? The whole thing's been gearing up for about six years, not less.

These are real things, the time for real action has come. Anyhow, that's enough.

Well, Kilt came out and said it, huh? It's true, it means it's all true – the time's come. It's approaching. It's time. What bloody God? He couldn't give a shit about this country, about these "God-chosen people". The people who spent the whole journey shoving stories down our throats about God loving Russia more than anywhere else – we'll sort those people out as well. It will be a serious confrontation: who said what, with what aim and why. Very serious. Enough. Enough of sitting and doing fuck all and just watching everything happen. From century to century – that can all go to hell – enough. Enough of all of that.

They'll say that it's terrorism and we'll say – yes! Yes, it's terrorism, but how else can we escape from you, from your mugs on the TV, from all of you? How long can we put up with you, you monsters, how much longer must our lives depend on you? How much longer will we die out under your wonderful speeches about stabilisation, the growth of the GDP and the journey towards the bright future??? You've pushed us too far, you've turned us into devils, into zombies, sent us into fits of vomiting, made our life unbearable, you're killing us, killing us, killing us!

God, if He saw everything you created, if He glanced over all of that and didn't do a damn thing – well then, He'll feel the same about what we'll do to you. He spat on your lives and he'll spit on your death. He spits on everything, simply because He can. He can, but we can't.

We're fed up, it's just all reached a critical mass, it's just – enough. Enough. All you have to do is take literally a couple of steps, so it all blows up, and you'll take them, we know that. We know that, sitting in Vladivostok and in Kaliningrad, sunbathing in Sochi, and freezing in the Kurile Islands, working and partying in Moscow and Petersburg. Our name is a legion, and you'll shriek in horror when you find out how many of us there are. At least, we'll do everything we can to make you shriek in horror. So think about your soul, think about God – He doesn't care about you, but you don't need to know that.

Just prepare to die.

That's the only thing.

Turning back, Timofei is replaced by Venya.

Venya I'm not even sure if . . . I know what I feel about this particular subject. Basically, I believe in God, yes, I believe in Him, but at the same time I can understand that it's . . . well, not that it's rubbish but that it's possible to get by, or whatever, without Him. You can kind of come to an agreement with God.

So, take "don't steal" for example, right? One of the commandments. And what if you're dying of hunger? Well, that's happened. And you go and steal. A bread roll, or something. Just some bread, ordinary bread. It's food – just to have something to eat. So does that make you a sinner? And if everything's in God's hands, then it turns out that God's appearing as a kind of agent provocateur – in other words, He's leading you into the kind of life where you'll be forced to break His commandments, and then you're going to be punished for it, is that it? How that works, I don't understand.

Or "don't kill". But if he comes at me first, and with a knife – because what he wants is to kill me? And let's say I grab a metal pipe – fully aware of what I'm doing – and give him a whack on the head, give that shit what he deserves, – then what? Is it a sin? I object! And he's writhing around and then lying there. Well, then what? It's all turned out as it should according to God's laws – should I have let myself be killed, or something? Like, "turn the other cheek" and so on? You accidentally squash that kind of monster, a thief, a real bandit – he was robbing you with a knife, do you understand?! – and you're a sinner? I somehow can't seem to make head or tail of this. In other words, what have I got to be sorry about? The cops were probably looking for him for fuck only knows how long – celebrations would be in order. He's crouching, ready.

The whole thing was an accident, an accident.

I'm not at all sorry, I don't feel it was any sort of sin, definitely not. I carried out His work, as it turned out. I'm not surprised He's not always there in time. He's all-seeing, all-hearing, but how many of us and how many of Him? He's sees everything, he hears it all, but

he can't always get there in time. So to duff up some sort of idiot –
that's a holy thing, I think. You wouldn't even be able to persuade
me to the contrary – my mind's made up.

He returns to his place, Kilt steps in where Venya was.

Kilt God exists but he's very tired. He worked hard, creating all
of this, and then improving it – or rather, he tried to improve it,
– but at some point, I believe, he just got tired. You could say he
washed his hands of everything. Now he's sitting, watching, and he
doesn't care. And the combination of his endless love for us with
this endless fatigue, which creates a desire to have nothing more to
do with us, makes him, in my opinion, the most unfortunate being
on earth. He's just a loving, very tired and really unhappy kind of
a guy.

I never thought of God as a wise old man with a grey beard, never
imagined him that way. Why should he be like that? It's just us
people who got used to it – if he's wise, it means he's an old man.
Of course not. Actually, he's very young. Maybe – my age. Because
for him the year-counter started ticking not that long ago and it'll
keep on ticking to the end of time.

I'm not sure what'll happen to him next. With his fatigue. Maybe
he'll get a second wind, he'll want to start doing something again.
Right now, he's just watching. I think he cries very often. Very
often. he sits, watches, and his tears are running and running . . .
That's what I think.

As it happens, I'm not upset with him. I even understand him in
some ways. It's just sometimes what's missing is his participation.
You sometimes think: "Help me, Lord" – but he's not there.
You might really need him sometimes, seriously, sometimes
desperately, not just for some rubbish: "Oh, Lord, help me pass
my exam with top marks!" – no. When you seriously need him.
When someone's not well. When you want to turn back the clock.
It's funny, isn't . . . Maybe, he's not crying after all, maybe he's
enjoying himself. Maybe, he feels amazing, to look at all of this.
He's created everything here and now he's just watching it. It's
one big game to him. Like "Quake" or "Dungeons and Dragons"
. . . except life's even more interesting. Yeah, he's got one hell of a
game.

If that's how it is, it means I'm a totally secondary character, of course. I might even be further down the list than that . . . But I do have some kind of a relationship with God. I mean, he must know I'm there. And that means everything's necessary somehow. It was necessary, for example, that in tenth grade Katka fell in love with me, so she had to ask her friend, Nadia, to bring me a note, because she was too shy to do it herself. That had to happen so that I wouldn't like Katka at all, but the opposite had to happen, I liked Nadia who brought me the note, so much that I . . . Well, it was necessary for me to fall in love with her like that.

I always need to find logic in everything, that's the point. But I don't see any logic here. I don't see any logic in this life. I don't understand why or how any of this happens. I don't understand why I should love a person so much that I'm afraid to tell her about it. I don't understand why I didn't say anything these four years. I just don't understand. An emptiness fills up my brains when I start to think about it. It fills up with "why?" "why?" "why?". And not a single answer. That's why there's me, there's Nadia, but there's no – us.

And now she has cancer, she's in hospital, and I can't go and tell her about all of this because she might think it's out of pity. Then she'll begin to hate me, because she's . . . she's proud, that's why.

And I'm an imbecile.

Why does God need all this, I don't understand?

Returning to his place, Sveta replaces Kilt on the front of the stage.

While she's speaking, the others comes up in turns next to her on the front of the stage.

Sveta   God? God. God. God – is God. What a word. Three letters in a row – gee, oh, dee. God. God. If you pronounce the first letter with a sigh and you rush "dee", then it's similar to Gob, and if you don't rush the "dee", you just deaden the "gee", then it's like "pod".

Gee. Oh. Dee.

For me, God's a combination of three letters because His name is a pale imitation of Him.

But "God" is just God: gee, oh, dee. Great Olympian Duck. Grassy Opulent Dirt. Gunman Out Diving. God is the Godly One Drifting and also the Glittering Orchestral Disease.

Timofei Gale Of Drought.

Venya Gluttonous Open Doctor.

Kilt Grief Ouzo Drops.

Sveta Goulash Offal Drink.

Timofei Giant Opaque Diaspora.

Venya Garage Open Door.

Kilt Grave, Oncology, Disease.

Sveta Glittering Occident Draw.

Timofei Gutter Over Dale.

Venya Greeting Old Danger.

Kilt Gabbling Orifice Dries.

Sveta Gogol Opting Dead.

Timofei Gliding Over Dreams.

Venya Guns Of Drums.

Kilt Greyhound Overtakes Dog.

Sveta God.

Timofei God.

Venya God.

Kilt God.

PART III

Nadia

Vitya

A hospital park. An alley, a bench. Nadia and Vitya are on the bench.

Nadia . . . And I hate it when she cries, you know? I hate it. What a load of bullshit, why should I put up with that? Her eyes are dry when she gets here, but it's obvious she's been crying!

Vitya Well, she is your mother . . . Mothers are always like that.

Nadia There's some tribe, I was reading about it, it was so cool: when a person knew they were dying, they'd get up and leave, wherever their legs took them. That's what dogs do, isn't it? They left, they died, properly – that's how it should be done.

Vitya " Properly" – how's that exactly?

Nadia It's by yourself. Alone. Each person dies alone – no need to clap, it's from some film. It's a quote.

Vitya Being alone is scary. I think.

Nadia Stop it. You're alone now – you're not scared, are you?

Vitya I'm not alone.

Nadia Well, I didn't mean literally. Obviously, you're with me right now. It doesn't even matter if you have parents or whatever, friends, that kind of thing, do you understand? I . . . I'm trying to make a metaphysical point, do you understand? Metaphysically, you're alone. Totally. Vacuum. Cosmos. And you. Do you understand? Totally alone. Imagine it. Because that's the truth of it.

Vitya I can't.

Nadia Well, try imagining. Believe in the abstract.

Vitya I can't. I'm not alone.

Nadia Hmph.

Vitya But it is terrifying.

Silence.

PART IV

Actress

Man

A dressing table in a theatre.

Actress My father taught me to keep my back straight, not to slouch. Do you see my posture? That's my dad. My father. He really loved history books. He read how they used to teach posture to some Austrian cadets or someone or other – they had to hold books under their armpits when they sat down to eat. That's how I ate from the age of five. In school, I used to stick up a head higher than everyone else in class: everyone stuck their noses into their exercise books but I sat properly, straight – like this. Mm. The teachers were always praising me but, I mean, I was so-so, not top marks or anything. But I had posture.

And when I auditioned for the academy, the panel said: "Oh, but you, my girl, you won't even need a corset on stage! Do you do ballet?" No, I didn't do ballet, however I lied and said I'd danced when I hadn't – I just loved dancing, I always danced all around the house, and everyone said I was good at it. So you could say I didn't lie – 'cos in a way I did dance, didn't I? And the panel thought ballet would be best, that's because of my posture, that's because of dad. Sometimes, when I lost it, he'd tap me on my back, meaning, straighten up: immediately, I go – zip – straighten my shoulders, pull in my stomach, bum out.

. . . My husband, when he got angry, would say that I don't bend at all in bed, as if I had a metal rod in my spine. In other words, all his delight withered into that one thing. 'Cos, at the beginning, when we met, because of love, he called me "countess" all the time, he said I looked like an aristocrat with my posture, he liked my arse sticking out, and this curve (*she touches her lower back*). But then he started banging on about – you know all that crap about the metal rod.

Where that came from! . . . human nature it's a fascinating thing. The process of emotional shrivelling never ceases to amaze me. Where does everything go, can someone please explain that? At what point does a "countess" become a "frigid slut", that's what I'd like to know. How do those little wheels, all the bits-and-bobs function inside our heads, eh? . . . I mean why? Why a "frigid slut"? Well, it's from the same hymn sheet as the spine like a rod. Another harmony, so to speak, but it's the same hymn. Oh dear!

What a great a singer that makes him. Hang on, he really was a singer. A lyrical tenor. Or baritone? . . . I'll be damned, I can't remember, shit. Completely forgotten.

We met at a festival concert. I was with my Mashka, doing our duet, he was separate. Songs of the Soviet composers. That was before perestroika, when everything was noble and honest, well, you remember. A suit, tie, a white shirt, eau-de-cologne "Sasha" – we bumped into each other backstage. Oh my God. But, you see, he didn't come with us in the bus – he took a taxi. He had just joined the philharmonic, we hadn't seen him before. Gorgeous! But I'm like already made-up and everything, Mashka and I were doing this eccentric dance, we've got tonnes of make-up on – makes us look like clowns – well, you've got the picture? And here he comes. So tall! I ran straight into him, looked up – wow. Look, I can't even explain . . . he's like drop-dead gorgeous, basically.

We were at the very beginning of the concert, he was at the end, after the concert they'd organised a philharmonic knees-up with our lot – that's where we met. He'd trained in the capital, can you imagine? Well, it was obvious from the first glance: he was a star! Because of his big city education, naturally, the head of the philharmonic sucked up to him, but he did have to lick the head's arse a bit anyway, oh his pride! My prince charming was so arrogant! What an education he'd had! You must be kidding. They were shouting left, right and centre at the philharmonic. And what do you think the head does? He's fawning over him, and then his favourite starts drinking, so all his performances are a frigging disaster, the head comes to me – sort out your husband! – but what can I do, you funny little man, are you having a laugh?! But my man, he can't drink quietly, he had to show off, hussar-style; there was that Vanka Kukharev, his buddy who was always sponging off him, eggs him on: "Stuff the philharmonic! You should go to Moscow!" Uh-huh. Brilliant idea. At least here he was a somebody, but what would he be in Moscow? He's a big fish in a small pond here, but Moscow's a big pond with a million fish like him in it. And you know he understood that perfectly, and he wouldn't even think about it . . . he was too afraid. But 'cos they kept on egging him on, he calls up the head drunk, when he's been with the lads, "Fuck you, I don't work for you anymore!" that was at the beginning, when they were drinking at night. Then it became

simpler, they started drinking in the day, as well, in broad daylight
in the philharmonic, in the head's office "Where's the vole?". The
head was a small, round and dark man, Valshtein, nicknamed
the Vole, and he knew that, too – well, and here comes my man
running around shouting about it at the top of voice like a right
pillock.

And the head fought for him, you know, really fought for him,
he loved him, valued him. My man is like – the "head of the
philharmonic's a homo, he was like hitting on me", but personally
I don't believe it because he was going off his rocker by then, his
life had gone down the drain after being fired. Yes, they fired him.
Because everything has a limit. I went in, of course. I'm crying, the
Vole is crying – and the upshot? Well, don't you think I realise how
much shit the philharmonic went through because of him? He was
a talent, what a talent, but it didn't help. Once, he even threw up
on stage, can you imagine? Br-r. During a performance! It was a
complete disgrace.

Well, of course, this was fertile ground for the rest of our
problems. And that's when it all started: "the metal stick in your
spine" and the "frigid slut", and many other wonderful things. The
only thing he did well – was he spared our child. In other words,
he'd kick up a fuss but quietly – you know, like, so Nadia wouldn't
hear. Sometimes, I'd start to raise my voice, he'd go – whack, on
my cheek: "Shut up! You'll wake little Nadia!" That was good, at
least. Nadia was already a big girl, she understood everything
going on, really. Sometimes, I'd be sitting with him, watching TV,
after we'd been arguing . . . she'd come over and sit down on the
sofa between us, take my hand, take his hand and put both our
hands on her lap. She brought us together like that. Symbolically,
so to speak. She was already twelve, a little princess. Thing is –
everything's clear to a child.

Oh, can you imagine. To bear all of his false airs, all his "Me!
Me! Me!"? Well, I'm also an actress, ladies and gentlemen. I also
have a delicate inner constitution *and* I have a higher education.
Not from the capital, of course, but not everyone can have that.
If his parents could afford to send him to Moscow, then, excuse
me, but I'm from the sticks, from Martinkin Hills, for your
information. If you step foot there, everyone in the village points
to our house: "What a woman lived here, now she's an actress in

the city, in the theatre, for your information!" It was easy: I got on the bus, two hours – there it was, the city, there it was, the institute. I'll be an actress, simple as that! And my young man at that time, in the village, Valerka Kislitsin, what did he say to me, when he sat me on the bus? "An actress is an arse-licker", that's what he said! The night before, he got legless, to try to stop me going, but he came to see me off anyway. He gave me his blessing, so to speak. Because he was so upset, of course. He loved me to bits.

But I was – no. It was my dream, my dream. From childhood, it was only that on my brain. They're specially put together our brains, us actors, do you understand that? Up here, everything is seen and imagined differently. It's um . . . everything's just different. It's here, it's here, it's here, it's all nerve endings, it's here, in our throats, as if there's a special vein beating inside you, vibrating. Me and Masha, my partner in the duet, talked a lot about that, 'cos she had the same thing, the same feelings and sensations . . .

Thing is – there was a whole other story, about me and Masha's life together, our duet. In other words, after some shots of vodka, we would talk about the noble craft of acting, about all of that "living and dying on stage", the whole malarkey, – after some shots of vodka we could talk about anything . . . but how, one wonders, were we going to buy more vodka? We had cameo roles in the theatre every other year – and the money? We're buying clothes . . . how exactly? We were young after all . . . o-oh, you wouldn't believe what Masha and I were like, no, you wouldn't! Always – like that! Hola! There we were – me a red-head, Masha a brunette; legs, bums, eyes – everything where it should be, thank God. We became friends in the institute, lived in the hostel together. Mashka was from the city, but she always had some argument or other at home with her parents, loads of relatives all living in two rooms, so she came to the hostel. And there was me. So that's how it all kicked off. Everything at once.

We graduated. So then what happened? I said I'd go to Moscow, to do the summer showcases. I saved up some money – my God. How many years, best not count. It's fine. I saved up some decent money. All of it went on the showcases. Because it was already obvious that nothing much was going down at our local theatres. Well, yeah. I went and did the showcases, got nothing and came back. Mashka screamed her head off: "I told you it was useless!". Get lost, I told her. I got really mad. Really mad because I still dreamed of Moscow, or at least somewhere nearer, maybe Petersburg. But, then, why go anywhere at all? It's all or nothing, I said to myself. But it was just after that journey, somehow . . . well, I don't know, I just decided not to go back. I'm totally stubborn really, "we walk forwards into the kingdom of freedom with our chests stuck out", hm, but actually . . . well, I don't know, basically. I decided not to go anywhere again.

So, I say to Mashka, how are you and me going to live now? There's nothing for us in the theatre, where will we get money? We sat down to think about it, and we thought up our eccentric duet. Well, it turned out there was nothing like it, so that's what we did. And it was okay – we pranced around for fifteen years, didn't kill us. I was the red-head in the blue blouse, Mashka – the brunette in the red blouse, we had eyebrows like this, cheeks here like this, lips.

If I didn't love dancing, I don't know how I'd have managed. Because of my posture, I always played someone important, while Mashka was always clowning around. Oh, my little Nadia, she was over the moon when she saw us perform! Well, children love it, you know. I've fed my family on that alone. In other words, my singer, with his baritone-lyrical tenor, well . . . children don't bloody need him. But us – yes, please. See, what his education came to? It's all vocals, but we use the Stanislavsky system, for your information. We can sing nursery rhymes on stage, or even turn into witches flying on broom-sticks, or play Nina in Chekhov when she's talking about her cross – it's all the same to us, we can do anything. But then my child says to me: "Mama, why are you prancing about on stage with aunty Masha like idiots?" "You what? Where did you get that into your head?!" – at which point my tenor comes into the room, with that crooked little smile on his face, and you know what he says: "Well, come on, answer the child. Let's hear from the great actress."

Well, I cried, of course. Of course. What do you think – is it possible not to cry after hearing that? But God's not an idiot. What goes around comes around. Literally, a couple of days went by – they gave me a role in the theatre. It was some rubbish about the collective farms but it was a big role, it seemed like there was actually something to play. The artistic director said to me I can do the best accent for the role, he was making fun of me, and two of the prima donnas start laughing – well, what do you know. It was set in my village Martinkin Hills, why else. I turned around, rotating with my straight spine, and from under my scarcely opened eyelids looked at the director, and with a voice emanating from the very depths of my diaphragm I said "I'm an actress and, if you want me to, Mr Principle Director, I can prepare the role of Lady Macbeth and I'll be ready to play it in one week in the original language." And well, it helped. I'm basically a simple person. I have a higher education, I've read a lot, I've read all of the Russian classics, I'm an actress, but all this affected behaviour . . . oh, I don't understand it. I can't bear it. I can't tell you how often I've seen it here. The prima donnas – ha, they have these fans, ha, they saved up and bought an antique screen, ha! Ha! Well, when you and I, the squirrel and the hare, are jumping around beside the Christmas tree – where's my screen, where my fan? Everyone needs to eat, so don't make such a haughty face, because you are playing in Chekhov, okay?!!

Well, whatever. I'm not bitter, not bitter at all, it's just sometimes it gets to me . . . It can be quite humiliating. Well, it's true, I'm not a star . . . it's not for everybody, it's not for everybody. I never allow myself to start feeling sorry for myself. Once you start doing that, it's all over. You never dig yourself out then. I look in the mirror, where's that little smile? There it is – I'm good to go. Here, there, everywhere, I need to work, to work – I need money, there's never enough money, never! There's no money. It became harder without Masha, of course, I don't have Masha now, and now I'm alone, it's harder. But it's fine, I'm earning money. Nadia needs medicine now, and it's essential to bring her nice things to eat in the hospital. Because I don't get any help from my ex-husband, he's been gone a long time – he went off five years to some distant relatives in the Crimea, he's some sort of guard there. He's given up drinking, at least, so that's something. Time to forgive and forget. It got to me so much all of that, our life together, the divorce was so awful – you can only cut yourself off from it. But that's all in the past. Go and be a guard there for the apricot trees, for all I care.

No, he's still a shit. If I could only send Nadia to the Crimea for the climate, with all the fresh air, the fruits, everything, but where would I send her? Has her father said where he is? How do people live there anyway . . . I don't understand. I don't understand. I mean, what's he thinking: his daughter's nineteen, she's basically grown-up, probably already working. So you know. Bastard, you bastard . . .

The door opens, a Man looks in.

Man Alla Vasilievna, we're beginning rehearsals.

Actress I'm coming.

Man We'll start from your monologue. "My father taught me . . . " et cetera.

Actress (*goes to the door, saying in a monotone*) "My father taught me to keep my back straight, not to slouch. Do you see my posture? That's my dad. My father. He really loved history books. He read how they used to teach posture to some Austrian cadets or someone or other – sitting to eat, they had to hold books under their armpits. I ate like that from five years old . . . "

PART V

Nadia

Vitya

A hospital park. An alleyway, a bench. Nadia and Vitya sit on a bench.

Vitya Have you had a bloke?

Nadia What?

Vitya Well, a boyfriend or whatever, I mean –

Nadia Yes, but never serious.

Vitya Me, too, with women, it's never quite worked out.

Nadia Yeah right.

Vitya It's true. I was forever getting nervous for some reason, I'd start muddling up my words . . . It's funny to talk about this now, isn't it?

Nadia Talk about it . . . if that's what you want.

Vitya Yes. So, I fancy you, for example. (*Nadia giggles.*) It's true! And if this wasn't here, but somewhere in real life, I would have made a move in your direction, yeah. Well, in other words . . . Well, we'd have probably, like, had a drink or, I don't know, gone dancing or something? Know what I mean? Candles, then wham-bam, in-out . . . I've never done it by candlelight, between you and me. I bought some once . . . there was this girl, Lena, and . . . well, anyway. Basically, I bought some candles. Red ones, can you imagine? Well, when Lenka arrived, everything flew out of my head. Candles, what candles? Don't forget to put on the condom . . . Shit! That's the kind of rubbish that would go round and round my head. I'm sorry. It's perfectly clear that nothing's going to happen between us, isn't it. 'Cos, I can't even kiss you, why is that? You understand, don't you? Well, perhaps as friends . . . Even then. You'd tell me to get lost, I suppose, end of story.

Nadia I'm deeply in love with one man. It was like this: my school friend fell in love with him, he was in the class above us. Well, so Katka, my friend, she was too shy – you know how it is with schoolgirls. Basically, she asked me to give him a note. And I fell in love like some sort of an idiot!

Vitya Cool. What did he do?

Nadia Nothing. Zero. He didn't even look at me. I should have told him, or what do you think?

Vitya Ring him and tell him. He can come over.

Nadia Uh-huh. He'll come running over . . . What, here?

Vitya Well, yeah, why not?

Nadia Come on. No, it's all over. It wasn't before but it is now.

Vitya Well, yes. These hospitals . . . men go funny in the head when they think about them.

Nadia That's what I mean. Do you know what I came up with? When I feel like I'm doing the final lap, completely diseased – I'll write him a letter. I'll write about my feelings. I'll ask my mother to send it to him, when I'm gone. That won't put any obligations on him, will it?

Vitya It's beautiful . . .

Nadia You wouldn't get upset if you got a letter like that?

Vitya No. It's actually quite romantic.

Nadia And it doesn't stop him from living, does it? He can do his thing, he's got his women whatever, parties – and suddenly this letter. Well, an omen with a message; maybe he'll crack open a bottle of beer for me, huh? Do you think?

Vitya I'd crack one open . . .

Nadia It's the best way out, I think.

Vitya Like in a novel . . .

Nadia Well, that's it then. It's been decided.

Vitya It's beautiful . . . The sun just doesn't give a damn, does it? (*He takes off his bandana and wipes the sweat from his brow.*)

Silence.

Nadia (*suddenly*) . . . And, you know, now, when everything's, well, finished, you have to understand that and accept it. Understand that you're totally alone, and that everything's finished and whatever you didn't manage to do, now you'll never do it. You've got to understand that, accept it and think only about that, you know? And that's the end of all stupidities. Your brain becomes . . . like ice, yes, like ice – transparent, clean, cold. A crystal clarity. Everything's clear. Everything's fine. Because if you waste time on all that rubbish: who you didn't fuck when you could have, whose face you should have smashed in, – then you'll climb up the walls and start gnashing your teeth. You'll waste your strength on the most meaningless thing – you'll pity yourself. You know?

Vitya What should you think about then?

Nadia Well, that's what I'm telling you: that you're alone, that everything's past and will never come back. That's what you need to think, the whole way, every day. Always. Everybody. Everything turns into sand and never comes back. You're here, you're now, at this moment and never again. And you're alone. And everything will end soon.

Vitya It's as if you're lying right in a grave.

Nadia Perfect! That's even better – just imagine that! As if everything's already over. Then you'll feel really good. (*She takes off her panama hat and fans herself with it.*)

Silence

Nadia and Vitya sit on a bench and each lost in their own thoughts.

The sun bakes their round, bald heads.

THE END

MUMS

(a play in one act)

by

Vladimir Zuev

Photographs. Letters.

Each mother has letters and photographs.

"Here little Seryozhenka's just one year old . . . "

"Here me and Kolya went to kindergarten . . . "

"Here me and Vanyushka became pioneers . . . "

"And here's Vitya at his school leaving . . . "

"This is Andriusha and me before being sworn into the army . . . "

I

The basement of an ordinary building. A criss-crossing of pipes. A bonfire burns by the entrance door. There are piles of planks, boxes, rags by the walls and women are sitting on them. One woman, a bit younger, than the rest is laying out cards. A second woman, a bit older, than the rest moves her hands over some photographs. A third burns some paper and watches the ashes. They are fortune-telling. Outside, there are explosions and gunfire.

The door of the basement flies open, the women huddle together on their piles of rubbish. A woman with a bunch of flowers walks into the basement. The woman smiles, crouches down near the fire. The women look at her for a long time and begin fortune-telling again.

Young Girl (*laying down cards onto a box*) Girls, I was taking a long hard look at us just now . . . We've gone nuts! Each one of us crazier than the other. And Verka's the craziest . . . (*Silence*) Verka, you did realise they were shooting right next to you, as you were taking your walk? Our whole basement has become your herbarium. Find your son – and *then* we'll pick flowers for him. (*She sits by the fire.*) What are you crying about?

Vera Yesterday I specially put a map under my pillow so I'd see where he is, in my sleep. One mum taught me that a year ago. That's how *she* was looking for her son. Then she was also killed. (*Pause.*) And I *saw* my Kolya. He was calling me, waving at me and shuffling along barefoot, leaving soggy foot prints on my map. Then he stopped and lay down. Like he was dead . . .

Old Girl You idiot, Verka! Don't say that till you've seen him with your own eyes. I've had three years of this, and they all say he's dead but in my heart of hearts I know he's alive. Did you see where he is? Come on, spit it out . . .

The women put aside their fortune-telling. They freeze, listen.

Vera He was so cheerful, kept laughing. And he waved at me. (*She starts crying.*) As soon as I woke up, I looked at the map – the one the soldiers gave me, and I saw that it's really near, so off I went. You were sleeping. And it's not far from here . . .

Young Girl Well?

Vera I was on my way, then they began shooting, I began to crawl a little bit, then there was an explosion right next to me.

Young Girl Did you find where he is?

Old Girl Can't you see that she can't hear you: it deafened – or shell-shocked her. Do we have anything to drink? (*Pause.*) Give us your flowers . . . I'll put them in water. (*She collects the flowers, puts them behind her back, hugs Vera.*) Go on have a cry. Tomorrow we'll go together – the two of us. Can I go with you? Well, what are you staring at, girls? Come on, gather up whatever you've got. There's a man who's promised to sell us three graves tomorrow morning.

Vera So many freckles on his face. He is a red-head after all. (*She gets out a bag from her coat pocket, pulls out letters and photos, looks at them and smiles.*) I'll find him tomorrow, I don't have the strength today. One soldier was telling me that he might have seen Kolya here, just where he was in my sleep –

Young Girl Drink up, Vera, it'll help you rest . . . (*Offers the cup.*) Have some of this, Rozka dragged over a whole barrel of the stuff, this morning. She even found a saucepan in the next door building – and two books. Drink up, and tomorrow we'll go out again.

Vera drinks, she cries, goes away to her pile. She turns up her things. She finds a topographical map, looks at the women, hides it under her clothes and lies down.

The women are quiet for a long time, drinking in turns, looking at the fire.

Rosa Maybe I should try the map too? If the mums are saying it works, then maybe it's true?

Young Girl What did you read in the ashes?

Rosa I mustn't tell you or it might not happen.

Old Girl It won't happen anyway.

Rosa (*to both Old Girl and Young Girl*) So why do *you* read the ashes? You've driven yourself mad doing it!

Young Girl Mind your own business! What else is there to do when they're shooting? You fall to pieces if all you do is read their letters. The ashes tell a different story each time.

Rosa Maybe she's already asleep?

Old Girl Forget the map, Rozka. Let the woman sleep it off. You can see she's not herself. Maybe she really will find him. I heard so many stories when I lived in the morgue for half a year. One mother from Moscow put her boy's army badge under her pillow at night. And she saw his ID number in her sleep. True – there was nothing left to bury: he'd been blown up by a mine . . . But she identified him. He'd had a large scar on his right hand since childhood. And that's how she identified him. She'd lived there a year. Washing the floors, doing the laundry. Then she found him and took him home. She came back and her husband had died. They missed each other by a month. Anything can happen. (*She drinks.*) And one boy kept coming to me. Not my own boy, though . . . He kept coming and saying: "Take me away from this place. Everyone else has been collected already, it's just me left. Thing are bad here, mum." And every night was like that . . . I was wailing and thinking to myself: "How can I take you back? Your own mum is looking for you. She'll turn up and you won't be here." (*Pause.*) One family took their son away. They buried him and after half a year the real parents came for him. They wanted to take their son back. And then they decided to visit the same grave, together. They're *all* children. (*Pause*) And they found *that* boy in the end, they took him back from the morgue.

Young Girl Old Girl, do you remember Svetka, who died? They took her son's bones and buried them. But she didn't believe it was him! She could *feel* that it wasn't her son. Her husband decided she was mad, he didn't let them open up the grave – so she came back again –

An explosion next to the building. The women lie on the floor. They lie there for a long time, not moving.

Old Girl Time to sleep. We'll leave early tomorrow, there's a lot to do.

II

Three small pits. Two soldiers lie in the pits. Kolya appears next to them.

Kolya Lads, got a smoke?

Andriukha Maybe you want some vodka, too?

Kolya I said I want a smoke.

Seryi No.

Andriukha Seryi, he doesn't get it, pretty funny, huh? Where exactly are you from, countryman?

Kolya Over there.

Andriukha That's where we're from! How about that, countryman! (*Laughs.*) Where did you live?

Kolya In Perm.

Seryi And I was in Samara. I'm Seryoga or . . . You can call me Seryi.

Andriukha Well, countryman, I was from Chelyabinsk. So we're both from the Urals, you and me.

Kolya Shame you've got nothing to smoke.

Andriukha And how were you planning to smoke? With your feet? (*Laughs.*) They've ripped off your pincers. Imagine it, Sergey, they've ripped off our countryman's pincers and he's there saying: something to smoke.

Seryi No harm in wanting. What's your name?

Kolya An APC drove over my arms . . .

Andriukha We don't care! What are you *called*? What name do you answer to? I'm called Andriukha.

Kolya I'm Kolya.

Andriukha As soon as I saw you, I knew right away you're a Kolya. We had one red-head in our class, also Kolya. Why are all red-heads called Kolya?

Kolya Where did *you* come from?

Seryi Why, do you prefer to lie by yourself? We're from *somewhere*, okay? We just need to look around and gather a crowd. Do you know how many of our lot are around here?!

Andriukha When our sergeant died, Seryi here took the command. He dreams of gathering an army now . . . (*Laughs*) Seryi, where will we deploy our red-head? Let's put him in the infantry, I mean, he's got legs. Kolyan, will you join the infantry?

Kolya I was in the mechanised brigade.

Andriukha Well – that's what you *were*. And now you're an armless corpse, that's why you'll join the infantry. I'm telling you as your commissioning officer!

Seryi Cut it out, Andriukha. (*Pause.*) Listen, Kolya. Since we've turned up here, we need to do something. Do you get it? Basically, you haven't yet been decommissioned.

Kolya But how will we get out of here? We're buried.

Seryi What are your brains for? Make an effort, think about it, warrior. Look into the earth, you'll see our boys. When you see someone, crawl over to him and start talking. We'll gather an army and we'll kick up some shit. Even in sub-Saharan Africa, a grave is still a grave, earth is still earth. I didn't get it at first but then this lieutenant explained it. Look and crawl. That's all there is to it, now.

Andriukha First time I saw Seryoga, I was confused as hell, same as you, but then I also fucking got it.

Kolya I'm not gonna crawl anywhere, they'll find me soon and then I'm going home.

Andriukha How will they find you! Other than us, who else knows you're here? Are you gonna have a party – lying there by yourself? I've been lying around a whole year.

Seryi The lieutenant told me that as long as you don't deserve to be found, they won't find you and you'll stay in the ground! You have to act in order to deserve it!

Kolya But what can we do? We're dug in!

Andriukha Seriously, ginger's a disaster zone in the brains department. Yesterday I shagged a local girl. Forget about your corpse. Brains – that's your strength! Imagine – and everything will be cool!

Kolya So can I smoke then?

Andriukha Finally – ker-ching! I mean, countryman, you're a retard! You can do *anything*! In fact, literally anything!!!

Seryi Quiet now, quit shouting . . . . ! They're coming towards us. (*They are quiet, listening.*)

Kolya They have to find me . . . (*Cries.*) Mum, I'm here, mummy!

Andriukha I'm here, mummy! Mummy!

Seryi Take me away from here, mum! Mummy, mummy!

"Mummy! Mummy! Mum! Mummy! Mum! Mummy! Mummy!"

III

Three small piles of stones. Around the stones are Young Girl, Old Girl and Roza. The women are sorting through the stones, digging the stony ground. Vera walks around in circles with a bunch of flowers, she smiles.

Vera Just like my dream. It's good I managed to pick the flowers yesterday. There aren't any here today. They were shooting all night – they got frightened and hid. They're scared. These flowers aren't pretty, like new-born babies. Only my Kolya was born handsome.

The midwife shows him to me and I'm afraid to open my eyes. I'm thinking he won't be handsome.

Rosa Vera, calm down. Go and help now. We can dig quicker while there's nobody around.

Vera But I'm afraid to look now, what if he's lying there, not handsome.

Young Girl If yours turns up, you'll take whatever you can get.

Old Girl I've dug up lots of strangers. Other mums turn up and take them back. How many of you boys have I dug up? If only my own –

Vera Kolya will be handsome, even there. But I'm still afraid.

Rosa (*to Young Girl and Old Girl*) Why do they call her "Vera-the-mine"?

Young Girl She used to wander around here when the war began. We found her dragging an anti-personnel mine around, shouting to everyone that it would blow up if anyone came near her!

Old Girl I had a gun at the start. It was really very scary but now . . . Who's interested in us?! You can see for yourself!

Rosa I thought I saw something . . .

All gather around Rosa's pit. Rosa digs out the earth with her hands, she pulls out a soldier's belt. The women stretch out their hands, they cry, they grab the belt away from one another.

Old Girl Stop grabbing it . . . Look inside, maybe something's written there.

Rosa Tell her to take her hands off it, I found it in my grave. (*Reads.*) "Welcome to hell". Nothing else.

Young Girl They all write that, I even had a photograph with Andriusha standing in front of a building and that's what's written on the photo . . .

Rosa Let's keep digging.

They dig the earth with their hands, throwing away stones.

Vera Dig, dig, look for yours, but mine is alive – live as a bird! He's not in the ground.

Rosa (*sits and cries*) And mine's alive, why am I digging? I've gone completely mad being with you lot. Mine only disappeared a year ago, why should I dig.

Old Girl Quiet, keep digging and cut the whingeing. "Yours, mine" – they've gone nuts. All of them are ours! I told you to dig! Please God nobody comes.

Young Girl I don't seem to have anything. Just a stone.

Old Girl Go and help Rosa, then. This one's empty too . . . (*She sits and cries.*) God, how many more empty ones . . . ? I'll be dead soon –

Young Girl I'll kill you myself if you don't shut up! You're the "Old Girl" here but only because you came to the war first, so don't start about your age . . .

Rosa They tricked us . . . There's nobody here, it's stone.

They sit, they are silent.

Old Girl We should mark this on the map so others don't come here. Verka, give me the map. (*Pause.*) Where *is* Verka?

They look around.

Young Girl She'll come back, she'll pick some more flowers and come.

Old Girl I feel sort of empty. Each empty grave I open – makes me want to hang myself. Why are we doing this? Huh? I've been wandering around here for three years. And there's nothing . . .

Young Girl We'll find them anyway.

Rosa Well, mine's alive! I'm an idiot, I should have waited at home, why did I start crawling around here. He's alive – and that's all there is to it! The thing is . . . during the day I'm certain he's alive but when night falls, it's like a light going out . . .

Young Girl Everyone feels like that.

Old Girl We'll wait for Vera and then we'll go back. (*Pause*.) God, I've been wandering around for three years, I've been wandering around here – but I'm still not used to it, not at all. (*Pause*.) You bastards!

Young Girl Bastards!

Rosa Bastards!

The women leave.

Vera is in a huge field of poppies. She touches the top of the flowers with the palm of her hands and smiles. She crouches down, gets her map and pencil. She searches for the spot and adds a cross. She pulls out armfuls of poppies. The flowers scatter from her hands. She takes off her coat and lays down the flowers in it. She takes the coat in her arms, like a child, and smiles. She shuts her eyes, sings a nursery rhyme, she gently sings. She walks along the field. There's a click. Vera freezes, she clutches the flowers, she crushes the flowers together. An explosion.

IV

The same basement. A bonfire burns. Rosa, Young Girl and Old Girl sit in their piles of rubbish. The first puts out the cards. The second moves her palm over the photographs. The third burns the paper and watches the flame. Flowers stand in a jar by Vera's pile of rubbish. The women are silent.

Rosa We've become really dull and nasty. We tell the future, we cry, we go searching . . . and then we start all over again. (*Pause*.) Well, Vera's not here anymore but everything's exactly the same. (*Silence*) If only something, anything would change.

Old Girl Go back home.

Rosa Why?

Young Girl Why stay here? (*Pause*) Forgive me, Rozka, but you came here in vain, you should have gone to the morgue, first. If he's not there, that means he's here. But you wouldn't survive there. I was white as a sheet after one week and I had to take my husband back home – he'd had a stroke. Every evening there, I drank spirits with the mums just – trying not go out of our minds. We laid out the children for burial, to the sound of our own wailing –

Old Girl Why are you getting hysterical?

Young Girl What I wanted to say is this: a doctor recorded some footage from the morgue, in exchange for my wedding ring. I've still got the footage. If I survive this place, I'll definitely show it to the "top brass". I'll sit down beside them personally and look at how they react to it when they're sober.

Old Girl Calm down, Young Girl! I've already asked you why you're getting worked up?

Rosa I'll learn from experience! And you know – I haven't seen that much less than you. Hospitals and military registrations . . . Anyway! It's *her* getting hysterical . . . ! Didn't the fortune-telling work out? Did yours turn out to be dead?

Old Girl Shut up, Rozka! We've just buried Vera and you start screaming. Try and remember who we can talk to, instead . . . about her . . .

Rosa We should look in her bag of letters. Shall I bring it over?

Young Girl Nothing stopping us now . . .

Old Girl Go on, bring it over, Rozka, my legs won't move anymore. We walked a lot today.

Rosa takes the bag from the empty pile of rubbish. They sit next to Old Girl, sort through the letters and photographs. They are silent.

Old Girl None of the letters have addresses. They say "my home" instead of an address and "for my mum" instead of a name.

Young Girl They weren't allowed to write home at all, to start with. They wrote letters and then hid them. She must have found them. They were in the barracks, probably. (*Pause*) Look, he really is a red-head. Looks just like Vera, a spitting image . . .

Rosa And mine's like his father, nothing from me except his character.

Old Girl Who can we tell? There's no address anywhere.

Young Girl Maybe we can go to the soldiers: they sometimes have journalists with them.

Rosa That's a long way to walk.

Old Girl We won't snap in half: we'll go. Young Girl, did you mark Vera on the map? We need to draw the spot again for relatives and give it to the soldiers. What if they start looking for her again, anything could happen.

They are silent for a long time, they look at the photos and the letters.

We should have put them in with Vera . . .

Rosa I keep thinking, why are we here? We walk around, looking for them. But what if we don't find them?

Young Girl Well, my son was walking, or is walking somewhere around here and breathing this foreign air, so I'm also breathing it and looking for him.

Old Girl You'll go mad quicker waiting at home but when you're here it seems like he might be alive somewhere nearby – or else he's already in the ground. If he ends up in the ground here, he won't rest peacefully.

Three small pits near to each other. Kolya, Andriukha and Seryi sit in the pits.

Kolya Lads, don't be offended.

Andriukha Go on, corpse-hero! Look – do you think we don't understand or something?!

Kolya We haven't seen each other for a long time . . .

Seryi Enough! You got how to crawl through, right? Go on, forward – just not for too long.

Kolya Well, I'll be off then?

Andriukha Right, well – good luck.

Seryi Listen, don't forget, we've still got things to do . . .

Kolya nods and disappears.

Andriukha When are they gonna find *me*?

Seryi Quit whining, it was chance. There was a mine field . . .

Two small pits near to each other. Kolya sits in one pit, Vera in another.

Vera You know what I remembered, son? You and I drank tea, the morning before the military commission . . .

Kolya Well . . . You're on about me rattling the cup with my spoon? I won't do that anymore.

Vera No, I looked at the cup, the way you were stirring the sugar . . . I was afraid to look into your eyes. And for the first time in my life I noticed that you stir sugar anti-clockwise.

Kolya As opposed to?

Vera That's what you said then! And it turns out, I totally forgot that you're left-handed, they made you write with your right hand at school . . . You wanted to stop time.

Kolya Eh?

Vera Nothing.

Kolya Mama, was it painful?

Vera The same as for you. And your papa died easily, in his sleep. He was a good man. Good children don't come from bad people.

Kolya Are we together forever now?

Vera I knew a few days ago that it was soon time but the mums didn't believe me. I'm lucky, aren't I?! Have I aged a lot? (*Digs in her pockets.*) Oh, I've become a complete idiot, I left your photographs and letters.

Kolya I knew you'd find them. Have you been here a long time?

Vera (*touches her son's empty sleeves*) I sewed you mittens and socks – true, I lost them later in a bombing.

Kolya I don't need any mittens now and the mosquitos are so tiny – and I can't rest peacefully in the ground here. Mama, mum, my mummy, I already stopped believing . . . (*Silence*) There are other lads here, besides me, waiting for their time to come. One's also from the Urals. So I'm lucky, even if I am a red-head. I was the first to be found! Hey, lads, didn't I say I'd be found soon?!

A plan flies low over the earth. Vera leans over to cover her son. Darkness.

V

The same basement. A bonfire is burning. Around it are Rosa, Young Girl, Old Girl and a journalist with a microphone. A man with a video-camera stands by Vera's old pile of rubbish.

Journalist Dan, did you get it all? Have a smoke. We can sit for a while, it'll quieten down outside and then we'll record some standing shots near the basement. (*Lighting up.*) This will create such a storm, mums! God Himself sent you our way! 'Cos the soldiers won't let us go anywhere. So, you actually live here? And there are just three of you, right?

Old Girl There were many more of us at first. Some left, some went to the morgue, we've lost so many. Vera was just killed. We told you about her –

Rosa Will they definitely show this?

Journalist Of course, they'll show it! When we get back, Dan will edit it and it'll be broadcast. Dan, it's warmer over here, come over here.

Young Girl We'd like to offer you to something to drink, pure alcohol. Rosa got it – she's the gatherer in our group. We just don't have a lot of food.

Old Girl Will you take some letters back home? Otherwise there's no other way we can get them back.

Dan Sure we'll take them, no question about it. Pure alcohol, you said? I won't say no. Lyolya, get out the canned food.

They drink in turns from the same cup, and they eat.

Lyolya Tell me honestly, not for the camera, do you believe you'll find them?

Old Girl Why would we be here otherwise? At least, there's *some* hope here. At home there's no work and no family.

Young Girl I wanted to hang myself twice, at home, and then I looked at the photos, I cried, I sold something and I came out here again. And now my husband's in the ground, I'm living like a nomad here.

Rosa Pity I didn't tell you about our military commissioner. He's a bastard! He was trying to persuade me not to come for a year, he said they're looking into it . . .

Dan Do they ever find them?

Old Girl Depends. If they're captured, they wait for an exchange or a ransom. But if they're not in the morgue or in the lists of the captured . . . they walk around, like us, looking for scraps.

Lyolya Isn't it frightening?

Young Girl It's worse at home. Old Girl and I have gone almost everywhere round here. We'll keep looking though. But generally the mums are only divided by hope.

Dan Sorry?

Old Girl Some have enough hope to keep looking. And to find them whatever it takes . . .

Rosa We didn't say much about Vera. We didn't even ask what her surname was.

They are quiet for a while, they drink.

Dan My battery has run out or I'd gladly film more.

Rosa Were you planning to record something else?

Lyolya No chance of that now. Pity we missed out on the standing shots. I keep wondering what to call the film. Maybe you can suggest something? It has to be something like "The fallen and the living" or "Between life and death", "On the Edge of Despair".

Old Girl Seems like it's got much quieter outside.

Dan Yes, they're shooting pretty lethargically. Right, time to go. Thank you for all the material.

Lyolya It's going to raise a storm, Mums, we promise you that. We'll see each other again, stay in touch. Good bye, all the best!

They go to the exit.

Rosa The letters, take the letters! You promised.

Dan We'll get them delivered to the right places, don't worry.

They leave. The women silently drink from their cups, they look at the fire.

Old Girl *All the material . . . .*

Rosa What?

Old Girl It would be better if they hadn't come. They've just scratched up everything inside.

Young Girl And what were you expect? *You* asked them to come.

Rosa Don't be silly, eh? What an opportunity for us! The whole country will see it! And then anyone who happens to know something, can write to us – and we'll find them . . . Let's go outside and get some air, they've almost stopped shooting.

Old Girl You go, I'm going to tell my future again.

Young Girl and Rosa leave. Old Girl gets out a photograph and looks at it.

Old Girl To hell with all of you! Bastards! Bastards! Bastards! (*Pause.*) What's this for?! When will it end?! God, it makes me sick to live like this! Take me quickly. You took my son, now take me . . . I can't go on, I've got no more strength. (*Pause*) Verka knew that there were mines in that field, that's why she went . . . My veins have all been ripped out of me . . .

Young Girl and Rosa enter.

Young Girl Let's go, we need to bury two boys. They're lying by the next building.

Old Girl Our boys?

Young Girl Theirs. But why should we leave them to lie there? Let's go.

Old Girl hides the photograph, wipes her face.

Young Girl You're fine like that, my beauty. Let's go before it gets dark.

They leave.

Dan and Lyolya are recording.

Lyolya (*into the camera lens*) Here we are at war, at the very centre of the events . . . We're at war . . . Why am I talking such bollocks? It was that alcohol! You know, they really got under my skin. Did you realise they've all gone nuts? Hey, don't record that!

Dan Lyolya, why don't we have children?

Lyolya I'm talking about work, as a matter of fact, in case you hadn't noticed?!

Dan Answer my question and then . . .

Lyolya *Then what*? *Why don't we have children*! What are you on about, Dan! I need a career! This is a like a fix, it's just so much material. Don't you want to aspire to a beautiful life? Do you want your whole life in this shit?

Dan I want children.

Lyolya So I'll have to leave home like them one day?! (*Pause*) Why bring children into this shithole? Give me one reason to bring children into the world?! I'm going to concentrate now, let's record this and go. I can't bear being here. (*Crouches down and cries.*) Those crazy old women! They've scared the shit out of me with their horror stories. "Little Kolyenka, Seryozhka, Andriushenka". We nursed them by day and by night, and then some bastards went – bang! – and we decided to play war-games. Simple as that!!!

Dan But we wouldn't let our boy come – if we have a son . . . I'd think up a million ways to keep him! *My son wants to go but I'm not going to let him*!

Lyolya Did you see their eyes? And that's not enough for you? It's enough for me, I don't want any more of this! If it wasn't for the alcohol, I wouldn't have made it out of that basement alive! There's nothing we can do for them. They've already got one foot in the grave . . .

Dan Lyolya, let's go home. We've done enough running around for material.

Lyolya It's okay – I'm alright. Let's record the standing shots and go. Turn the light on or you won't see me properly.

Dan switches the camera light on. Lyolya looks at the mirror. She wipes away her tears.

We're at war. Here, every day, men, fathers and sons are dying. Today we were fortunate enough to meet –

A shot. The light goes out. Dan looks with surprise at the camera, he falls. Lyolya runs to him, shouts.

VI

The same basement. Rosa, Young Girl, Old Girl and Lyolya are around a bonfire. Dan's body lies by the entrance.

Rosa It was a sniper. They turned a light on so a sniper goes and shoots.

Old Girl Quiet Rozka – pour us something to drink. (*To Lyolya*) Have one more sip and then try to sleep. You need to warm up. You've been lying there for almost two hours. We were burying the boys then we heard you. (*The cup falls.*) Come on, don't be stubborn. (*Lyolya drinks, coughs.*) Tomorrow we'll go to see the soldiers, they'll take him back. Do you have children?

Lyolya shouts, cries.

Young Girl, let's put her on Vera's bed, she needs to sleep.

They take Lyolya under the arms, lead her to the empty pile. Lyolya buries her face against the wall.

Young Girl We shouldn't have asked them to come. She'll never forgive us, not in her whole life.

Rosa Who knew that would happen? And he went and did a smart thing: turning on the light!

Old Girl You can go to see the soldiers tomorrow morning and I'll stay here with her. It's time to sleep now. Put out the fire.

Rosa What about her?

Old Girl She'll fall asleep in a while. I'll keep an eye on her. Go on, lie down.

The women lie down. The fire goes out. It's dark. Crying.

Andrei, Sergey, Kolya and Vera are walking in the basement. They are looking at the faces of the sleeping people.

Vera Here they all are!

Sergey Yes, here's my mum sleeping.

Andrey And mine . . . Quiet all of you . . .

Kolya We *are* being quiet . . .

Vera They can't hear us. When I was with them, I didn't hear anything, I only *felt* certain things. Something would be hurting inside. You can look at them but let them sleep. They've got a lot to do tomorrow . . .

Sergey My mum's grown so old.

Andrey And mine's already gone grey. She's got thin. She tried to lose weight every year in time for her birthday. It never worked and she'd get angry and not eat anything. (*Stands by Lyolya.*) Here's a nice young one –

Dan Back off, that's my wife.

Andrey And who's this talking corpse?! (*Goes over to Dan.*) Who are you, warrior?! (*pause*) Sergey, there's a civilian here, a really odd one!

Dan I'm Daniel.

Andrey You *were* Daniel, anyway.

Kolya That's enough, lads, let him get his bearings. Were you killed a long time ago?

Dan They were shooting at me this evening –

Andrey What's that you're mumbling, one-eye?

Sergey Quiet! Our mums need to get some sleep.

Andrey Look at this, what a sightless wonder we have!

Vera They can't hear.

Dan Lyolya . . .

Kolya She's beautiful, your girl . . .

Dan Lyolya, can you hear me?!

Sergey Shut your mouth, cripple! I'm in charge here.

Andrey Here we go!! *Here's* my *mum, I've found* mine, *now you get lost,* it's each to his own now . . .

Silence.

Sergey (*To Andrey*) Bastards, they put you on a mine . . .

Andrey Ginger's with his mum now but what about me?! Come on, tell me the options, commander . . .

Sergey Do you want to take her away? Don't you feel bad?!

Andrey And you don't want to?

Sergey Me – no!

Andrey No need to *cure* me, got it?!

Sergey Let her think I'm alive. Do you know what I was up to before the army! I made her a nervous wreck the whole time.

Andrey Well, I don't want to be here anymore. I want to go home. I'm fed up with all of this –

Sergey You'll stay, alright?! Who's going to look for new warriors with me? (*Pause*) Okay . . . who wants to stay?

Kolya Mum and I are staying . . . Where would we go?

Sergey And you, journalist? What are you hanging around for? . . . Let's go crawling together! We'll make some real films you and me!

Dan My camera's still . . . – where we were filming.

Sergey No need, Dan! Get used to it right away. Say it: "Where I was killed". Say it!

Dan It's there –

Andrey Don't be offended, Seryi! Me too, it gets stuck in my throat, you know.

Sergey (*to Andrey*) Don't bury your mum. It was an accident with Kolya, believe me. (*Pause.*) Let's go, journalist.

Sergey and Dan disappear. Andrey sits at the head of the bed with Young Girl. Kolya is with Vera by the fire. It's quiet. The only noise is Lyolya's crying.

VII

The same basement. Around a bonfire – Rosa, Young Girl, Old Girl. In the corner – Vera with Kolya and Andrey.

Old Girl It's happened before. They carried off the bodies and bury them, then they ask for ransom. We need to search for it and if we don't find it – then we wait for a letter or a person.

Rosa I've not heard of that before . . . Where will they bury him?

Young Girl They'll find somewhere! There's nothing they won't do for money!

Silence.

Old Girl And where did the girl go? Maybe she carried it off?

Rosa He was a big guy –

Young Girl I've lugged around some humanitarian food bags, it was okay.

Old Girl We should go.

Rosa She came to, and went off to see the soldiers. Young Girl and I will go and you wait here: she might suddenly come back.

Old Girl Yeah? Just make it quick, alright!

Rosa and Young Girl collect their things and leave. Old Girl takes out letters and photographs. She reads the letters.

Vera And we're here like this every one of God's days . . . Searching, crying. Reading, crying.

Andrey I'll go after my mum. Why did they go just the two of them?! (*He leaves*)

Kolya Come on, mum, don't you start crying now! That's enough . . .

Vera You got ill when it was almost the New Year – you were only one year-old – and you were breathing through your mouth. You had a blocked nose. You kept on crying. And I didn't have any medicine for your nose, nothing to hand. So I sucked out your snot with my mouth. (*Pause.*) And you calmed down, you stopped crying. You fell asleep and started smiling.

Kolya Why did you do that? I would have got better anyway –

Vera Of course . . .

Kolya What will happen to them all now?

Vera Who knows?!

Kolya Mum, did you know the mines were there?

Vera First I had this dream . . . and when I saw the poppies, I forgot about everything else. You should have seen the field! It was bright red, off into the horizon . . . I was walking, further and further and then – the explosion, then I saw you immediately.

Silence.

Old Girl (*reading a letter*) "Mum, you remember someone knocked down all the shelves in the basement and broke the jars of your homemade jams. Don't swear too much at me, it was an accident. I was looking for homebrew. We had a party at school. Then the lights went out again and I crawled down there, with matches. I burnt my fingers and I hit the shelves with my hand. It's beautiful, here. There's probably still snow at home but here the flowers are still in full bloom. Yesterday they gave us a new uniform. The soldiers about to be discharged say it's for travelling.

So they're sending us somewhere. At least I'll get to see the world. How are my buddies?! Did Vityok get accepted into the architecture department? Okay, time to go on guard duty. Kisses and hugs. Mum, the main thing is, don't cry, I've got to survive one winter – and then I'm coming home. Bye. Your Sergey."

Kolya Mum, do you remember, the money which went missing from the shelf? I took it. I really liked Svetka from the class next to mine and I bought her lots of flowers for the eighth of March. But she kissed Tolyan at the school leaving. I'm sorry that I'm only telling you now. (*Pause.*) Do you know how she's doing?!

Vera She rang a couple of times to ask where you were and how you are . . . That was before the war . . .

Kolya I'd like to take a look at her now! She's probably really good-looking. (*Pause.*) Mum, why did she read the letter out loud?

Vera To give it expression. You read out loud when you want to see how your son wrote the letter. I used to see you open your mouth and speak the things you wrote. And she sees her son. Around other people we read to ourselves – but when we're alone, we always read out loud.

Kolya Interesting. I never would've thought that's important.

Vera I carried your things with me the first year. At night, I buried my face in your knitted jumper . . .

Kolya The one with the neck? I burnt that one with a cigarette –

Vera I'd start bawling – as it gets to morning I'd wring it out. But then there was a bombing (I ran out from the basement with the mums) and I forgot it. I threw everything down – absolutely everything in the rush to get out. We came back the next morning but the building was bombed to pieces and everything was burnt . . .

Old Girl lies down. She buries her face in the scattered letters. She says a prayer. Vera and Kolya sit beside her. Vera strokes her head. Kolya look at his empty sleeves. Old Girl lifts her head, looks through Vera and Kolya. She jumps up and runs out of the basement.

VIII

The same basement. Young Girl and Old Girl are by the fire.

Young Girl They had to use force to persuade Lyolya to tear herself away from his body. She clutched onto him – she was wailing. The soldiers were standing around her, they couldn't do anything. Rozka went straight away into the headquarters. She runs out of there, shouting. There are new exchange lists in the headquarters. Her Vanya's on the list. He's been captured. So, she stayed to wait for the exchange. (*Pause.*) Where should we go now?!

Old Girl Ours weren't on the list?

Silence.

Young Girl So it's just the two of us. It's so depressing now. Rozka's stern, but it was still more cheerful with her. It *is* true, after all – three is better than two.

Old Girl It felt like Vera had come back. I was reading and crying. I had buried my face in the letters and it was as if someone was lightly stroking my hair. When she was alive, Vera was always stroking my hair. (*Pause*) Did you find anything out about Andrey?

Young Girl Do you remember last year I was handing out photocopies of him to everyone, – the colonel had made them for us from the photos. One soldier – who's working in a private army now – saw Andriusha. He says they were carrying him. He was heavy, wounded in the chest. They left him in the field hospital. It was after a tough battle.

Old Girl So is he alive?

Young Girl I don't know. He showed me the place on the map where the field hospital was. I'll go tomorrow.

Old Girl We'll go together.

Young Girl No, I'll go alone. Don't come with me, there's no need.

Old Girl We've been together the whole war but now it's "don't come with me"!

Silence.

Young Girl I should go alone. I've coped alone, I carried him inside me alone, I gave birth to him alone. And now I'll go alone. Sorry, Masha.

Old Girl Masha. I haven't heard my own name for so long. You're right. You're right. I'm afraid to be alone. It's like I've only just got here. I've always got this fear, like something is happening, but when I'm alone . . . You're like a sister to me. Don't leave me.

Young Girl Tell me you wouldn't go! You'd go! I'm tired. I'm so tired I've gone grey. We'll have a good night's sleep and I'll go in the morning. It's not far according to this map.

Old Girl You can't imagine how pleased I was about Vera. Like being with my mum when I was a child, her stroking my hair. You want to curl up in a ball because your mum's next to you.

Young Girl Feels like I've already seen *everything* but I can't imagine Andriusha dead. However much death I've seen, I still can't. Can you?

Old Girl I saw him once in a dream. But he's alive and still here!

Young Girl Here, take this ring. The girl gave it away, the journalist. Said she didn't need it anymore.

Old Girl It's only good for fortune-telling . . . And how did she carry his body, she's such a slender thing?!

Young Girl We should go to church. Shame there isn't one here. And the priest only flies in to see the soldiers every other week.

Old Girl So we'll go, I've been planning to go for ages.

Young Girl I've lost my cross somewhere. I only noticed today. That's a bad omen. Andriusha and I bought it together when he was christened. I've lost it somewhere. The thread was so old.

Old Girl The priest will probably have some: he blesses the boys after all.

Young Girl I wanted to ask you: tell me the parable about the black and white lines. Do you remember it?

Old Girl I've already told you a hundred times. Why do you want that one?

Young Girl It's beautiful.

Old Girl Once upon a time there was a woman. She was happy. She had a home. She had a husband. Then came the war. Her son went missing. Her husband died. She searched and searched for her son. He wasn't anywhere to be found. She suffered so much and said to God: "Lord, why does this happen? I had everything and now I've got only emptiness". And God answers her: "You see the white line. And after it – the black line. On the white line there are two sets of footprints, and on the black one – only one." The woman asks: "Whose footprints are those, Lord?" God replies: "When you're on the white line, I'm walking alongside you". The woman thought about it and started bawling: "And in grief I walk alone?!" And God replies: "You idiot, that's when I'm carrying you in my arms!".

Silence.

Young Girl "I'm carrying you in my arms . . . " You should dictate that to me and I'll copy it out. It might come in useful, I can tell it to someone when they're in trouble. I meant to do that a hundred times already but it was never the right time. I'll write it down now.

IX

In the basement, Sergey, Dan and Andrei sit by the fire. Dan smokes. Old Girl and Young Girl sleep.

Sergey So, home – tomorrow.

Dan They're sending Lyolya and me back on a plane. Our business trip is over, well and I was . . .

Andrey Say it like any other person: "Killed!" Go on: k-ill-ed!

Dan Fuck off. Killed or not killed – I'm dead either way!

Sergey Will the film still be made?

Dan I don't know whether Lyolya –

Andrey She'll get over it, surely. Not immediately, of course.

Sergey It would be a great film! Instructive and educational! Well, it's best that you're off. What here's for you, as a civilian? We're the soldiers!

Dan I still don't understand how you're planning to fight? Have you gathered an army?

Sergey Mentally! Ideas are power! If you really want something then it happens! When you've got a body, you don't particularly have to exert your brains. You stretch out your hand and take it. So you have no power in your brain! But try taking it without your body! Then your brain really begins to toil! It's hard at first but what can you do?!

Andrey Using his method – I even shagged a girl!

Sergey Don't listen to him, he's flipped when it comes to that.

Andrey Well, that's 'cos when I was alive, I didn't make love to a single girl, so . . .

Sergey Why are you blushing? It's a shame! But now you can do it with any –

Dan For you lads!

They drink in turn from the same cup.

Andrey My mum will go looking for me again tomorrow. And I'm lying on a mine! How can I lead her in another direction?!

Sergey Appear to her in a dream and tell her that you're not lying there. I'm telling mine that I'm alive all the time. Captured – I tell her.

Andrey She won't believe it. A private army guy even showed her where the military hospital was on the map, the bastard.

Dan While we were doing interviews, I heard so many stories my hair stood up on end. They put up with so much for us! If I were in their place, I'd have been locked up in a madhouse a long time ago.

Sergey If my mum's left alone, she won't manage. They're like sisters, mine and yours.

Andrey And we've been like brothers for a long time.

Sergey So you get on to it, think something up – get ready to start lying.

Andrey I've got a problem with that. I'm not able to make stuff up like you. (*Pause*) She knows that I'm already dead. She's known it for ages.

Dan And what will you do next?

Sergey Let's see. We need to smear the brains of the politicians. Imagine if the full force of a dead army piles into your dream like a living person. In full force! Every night! And we begin to whisper threateningly: "Lead the troops out of here, you bastard! Or else you're going to have to fucking kill every single person here!" We can interfere with all their brains.

Andrey So they'll know that being at war isn't like being on a woman!

Sergey How do you know what *that*'s like? (*to Dan*) So that's how I see our war. You can take part, by the way. You didn't manage it alive, don't miss your chance. You'd be a visible spokesman for us.

Dan (*covering his eyes with his palm*) Will you remind me my whole life about my eyes? That's enough, lads.

Andrey What's so scary about it, one-eye! Don't be offended, you're among friends.

Young Girl quietly gets up. She looks at the map. She gets her things and re-reads the letters. She looks at the photograph for a long time. She puts everything carefully into a bag, puts it onto her pile. She sits beside Old Girl. She strokes above her hair without touching her. She stands up and crosses Old Girl. She leaves the basement.

Andrey Seryi, what should I do?! We've been talking, I didn't have time to . . . Now what? Don't stay silent, you bastard! Who's in charge, you or me?!

Sergey Let's go after her, maybe we'll think of something. Are you coming, Dan?

Dan Lads, my plane is in an hour. Don't be offended, eh!

Sergey   Okay, good luck. Join us later if you can.

Sergey and Andrey leave. Dan drinks, smokes. He looks around the basement, sits down by Old Girl, strokes her hair. He crosses her and leaves.

X

Young Girl is by a small pit. She digs the earth with her hands. Andrey and Sergey stand besides her.

Andrey   Well, think of something already! Mum, mummy, don't dig here! That filthy private soldier. I'll string you up by your balls, you bastard. Mummy! Mum, don't do it. Don't go there!

Sergey   There's no point. She can't hear you. She's made up her mind, she said goodbye to my mum yesterday. She left your letters. Maybe it will be easier for her. They're completely drained.

Andrey   Mum, mummy, mum, I'm alive, I've been captured! Get away from here! When they dumped me, they put a mine under me. Go away, mum.

Andrey tries to push him mum away from the pit. He pushes the air, shouts, cries. Sergey turns away, looks at the sky. He frowns. He crouches down, curls into a ball, clutches his head with his hands. Andrey kicks Sergey, shouts. He falls onto the ground. They both shout.

"Mummy! Mummy! Mummy! Mummy! Mummy! Mummy! Mummy!"

Young Girl seems to hear them, looks at the sky and cries.

XI

A long wooden table in the field. Along both sides of the table are benches. Samovars and glasses on the table. On one side of the table sits Old Girl. On the other side: Vera, Kolya, Sergey, Andrey, Young Girl. Dan and many other boys are in uniform.

Old Girl   So the white line happened, didn't it, Young Girl?

Young Girl I look at Andriushka and I can't stop feeling happy. I've never seen him so grown up. I'm better here, Masha.

Old Girl Seryozhka, sit next to me. I'm tired without you, son.

Sergey Mum, I have to sit in the right place. That's how someone's decided it has to be. I can't sit beside you.

Old Girl And why did you lie to me, in my dreams – you told me you're alive?! I punished you harshly for lying when you were little.

Andrey Auntie Masha, he wanted to do the best by you.

Young Girl Don't get involved. Look at you, a defender of the people!

Vera Don't swear. Today's a celebration!

Old Girl What celebration, Vera? A religious holiday?

Sergey Happy birthday, mummy. You forgot about yourself with this war. I wish you good health and I'm asking you: please go home already.

They all take their glasses and shout: "Happy birthday! Happy birthday! Happy birthday!"

Old Girl But how will I go home without you?

Kolya When the war ends, you'll come back and get him!

Old Girl When will it end?! I won't live to see that. I should bury you – and my soul would be at rest. Young Girl came later than me and she's already at rest. She's just glowing. (*To Young Girl.*) I knew that you were saying farewell to me that time . . . You tidied up your letters, I'm keeping them with mine.

Young Girl Do you know what I'll ask you to do. Take my video from the morgue to the right places, let them see what they've created.

Old Girl If I'm still alive, I'll pass it on. (*Pause*) So, Seryozhka, you're in the ground.

Sergey Mum, I'm waging my war here. One clever person told me that when your time comes they find you. But I haven't yet done everything.

Dan   Let me photograph you for memory's sake. I'll stand back a bit so both sides fit into the frame.

They all look at Dan and smile. A flash.

Old Girl opens her eyes. The basement. She puts Young Girl's letters and photos together with her own. She takes out the photo of her son. She smiles.

XII

The basement. Old Girl writes a letter by the fire. She speaks out loud what she's written.

Old Girl   "Hello, son. Yesterday I lost my sister, Young Girl. She found her Andriushka but she was killed herself. A mine was lying under him. I knew it would turn out that way. I wanted to stop her but I didn't have the strength. Tomorrow I'll fly home to carry them back. The soldiers promised to take all three of us by plane. Thank you for reminding me about my birthday. I wouldn't have remembered it, at all. I've decided: until I find you, I'll write you letters and dig them into the earth so they reach you quicker. I know you'll get them and read them. I need to go to Moscow – my sister left me some footage from the morgue. Maybe it will get through to the authorities. I'm tired here, son. It's really unbearable, being alone. What can I do here alone? So I'll fly home and then let's see. I'll keep looking for you until I die. This isn't right – for you to lie in a foreign land. It's just not right. We had one woman here, Rosa. She found her boy. If I could, I'd take everyone away with me – every single one of them. Also I thought of putting up a statue in our town for all of you. We'll collect money from the mums and put one up. Maybe I'll get someone in Moscow to agree to it. I have so many sisters across the whole country now. Okay, I think I've told you everything for today. I'm going before it gets dark. I love you, I remember you. Your mummy."

She carefully folds the letter. She puts it in a polythene bag. She goes outside. She digs a pit. She puts the letter down and buries it.

XIII

The basement of an ordinary building. A criss-crossing of pipes. A bonfire burns by the entrance. By the walls, there are piles of planks, boxes, rags. Women are sitting on them. One is laying out cards. A second moves her hands over some photographs. A third burns some paper and watches the ashes. Outside, there are explosions and gunshots.

The door of the basement flies open, the women huddle together into their piles of rubbish. Old Girl comes into the basement. She smiles, crouches down by the fire. She pulls out a photograph from her pocket, and an exercise book and pen. She looks at the photograph, writes in the exercise book. The women look at her for a long time and begin fortune-telling again.

THE END

PERFORMANCE NOTES

The translations presented in this collection are the performance drafts of the plays as presented by Sputnik Theatre Company in London, with small edits and adaptations from the original, where appropriate:

Slow Sword by Yuri Klavdiev was presented by Sputnik Theatre Company at the Old Red Lion, 20 November to 8 December 2007.

Dreams by Natalia Koliada was presented by Sputnik Theatre Company at Soho Theatre, 1 February 2010.

Tityus the Irreproachable by Maksim Kurochkin was presented by Sputnik Theatre Company at Soho Theatre, 2 February 2010.

Techniques of Breathing in an Airlocked Space by Natalia Moshina was presented by Sputnik Theatre Company at the Old Red Lion, 15 August to 19 September 2006.

Mums by Vladimir Zuev was presented by Sputnik Theatre Company at Soho Theatre, 3 February 2010.

ABOUT THE AUTHORS & EDITOR

AUTHORS

Yuri Klavdiev has written numerous plays staged in cities across Russia, including Moscow, St Petersburg, Perm and Togliatti. Productions include *Sobiratel' Pul'* (*The Bullet Collector*) at the Prakitka Theatre (2006) and *Ya – Pulemyotchik* (*I'm a Machine-Gunner*) at Teatr.doc (2007). He also regularly writes for television and film, including episodes of the iconic TV series *Shkola* (*The School*) (2010). Klavdiev is also a professional rock singer.

Natalia Koliada is co-founder of the Belarus Free Theatre. The company's patron is Sir Tom Stoppard. Her company is banned from working in their home country, although for many years they worked "underground" in Minsk, while also touring their work abroad. Koliada's company is now based in London. Over the years, Free Theatre has had plays at the most respected British new writing theatres, such as the Soho Theatre, the Young Vic and the Almeida. *Im Snilis' Sny* (*Dreams*) was Natalia's first play.

Maksim Kurochkin was born in Ukraine but now lives in Moscow. He won the Anti-Booker prize for "innovation in playwriting" ("*Za poisk novykh putei v dramaturgii*") in 1998. His play *Kukhnya* (*The Kitchen*) was produced and acted in by Oleg Menshikov, one of Russia's best-loved film stars, in 2000. He has written numerous plays and films, and also works as an actor. He is on the organising committee of the prestigious Lyubimovka Festival of Contemporary Drama in Moscow.

Natalia Moshina made her debut at the Lyubimovka Festival of Contemporary Drama in 2004, and has subsequently had twenty productions both in Russia and abroad, winning numerous playwriting awards. Her play *Zhara* (*Heat*) continues to run in rep at the Praktika Theatre in Moscow. Moshina studied psychology at university. She lives and works in Ufa, in central Russia.

Vladimir Zuev wrote *Mamochki* (*Mums*) in 2006, winning the Eurasia Award, and bringing him immediate attention. The play has been presented in thirty-five theatres or professional drama schools across Russia. Since then, he has written twenty plays, many of which have won awards or been published in journals, including the prestigious *Sovremennaya Dramaturgiya* (*Contemporary Playwriting*).

TRANSLATOR/EDITOR

Noah Birksted-Breen is founder and artistic director of Sputnik Theatre Company, the only British theatre company dedicated to bringing Russian-language plays to British audiences. As a director, Noah won the Channel 4 Theatre Directors' Award, working for a year and a half as resident director at Hampstead Theatre, where he trained alongside some of Britain's top theatre directors, including Rupert Goold, Polly Teale and Lucy Bailey. Noah has directed eight productions in fringe and off–West End venues.

Noah speaks fluent Russian: he holds a Modern Languages degree from Oxford University, which included one year studying at the St Petersburg State University, and he completed an MA in Playwriting at Central School of Speech and Drama. He has qualified as a professional translator, gaining a Translation Diploma in 2011 from the Institute of Linguistics, with Merit (General Paper), Distinction (Literature), Distinction (Law). Noah has translated over a dozen plays from Russian, as well as a variety of academic books, short stories and poetry.

Noah is currently studying for a practice-based PhD on "Alternative Voices in an Acquiescent Society: Translating the New Wave of Russian Playwrights", funded by a British government bursary (AHRC), at Queen Mary, University of London, in partnership with Theatre Royal Plymouth. Noah has also been a freelance Artistic Assessor for the Arts Council England since 2010. With Christine Bacon, Noah also co-authored *On the Record*, which was produced by iceandfire theatre company at the Arcola Theatre.